The Jo[ur]... from from Orphan to Soke

by
Frederick Douglas Peterson

DEDICATION OF THIS BOOK

The authors of this book, Frederick Peterson, Danny Layne and Thomas Hardie would first like to honor God for allowing us to share and enjoy what we have been fortunate to do in the martial arts for many years. Much thanks is due to Angela Hardie for her countless and tedious hours devoted to the assisting of the transcribing of audio and handwritten notes. Pardon the cliche but this book project was truly a labor of love. It involved many hours of effort, late nights and multiple trips to the Peterson home in Arizona. We also take time to honor our family members, living and departed that supported us through the blood, sweat, injuries, sacrifices and victories in our lives. Additionally we are thankful to all who have been a part of our lives in some way from our mentors, friends and acquaintances and martial arts family who all contributed to this story in some way. Lastly, we are grateful to the man who lived the life, the history and provided the service we are about to share with you.

ISBN:978-0-9829926-5-4

Published in the United States by
Five Birds Publications,
For Heroes' Hearts® Inc.
8112 Terracotta Gulf Ct. Las Vegas NV 89143

This book is not intended as libelous, slanderous or to caste a negative pall on any person either living or dead. The story is completely derived from first person recordings and writings. Any opinions or statements made by the narrators, therefore are their responsibilities.

Edited with Foreword by Thomas Hardie
Cover Design by Jessie Horsting

Contents

Foreword
by
Thomas Hardie

Soke Peterson and Grandmaster Hardie having fun in a kiba dachi (horse stance) with a bit of meditation during a 2018 summer day in Gilbert, AZ.

It was October 1984 that I first made the acquaintance of Frederick Douglas Peterson Jr. who I would discover was a well-respected master of the martial arts at the time. I would later come to find out that he had developed his own style which is called Tai-Chi Jitsu. At the time I was a few months removed from college graduation at CSULB and I worked out at a fitness gym located in the Wrigley area of Long Beach, CA.

It was there at the gym that I saw 59-year-old Master Peterson lifting weights while wearing his Tai-Chi Jitsu t-shirt. I was curious and asked him if he taught locally and he said yes. It was on. I had long wanted to train in the arts and he invited me to his dojo. This was a far cry from my last year at James Denman Junior High School when a couple friends of mine and I would attempt to imitate moves that we had just seen in Kung Fu movies, Friday nights at the old Grand Theater on Mission Street in San Francisco, CA.

Training with Master Peterson however was the real deal. No imitating of moves viewed in a film but learning real self defense. At the time when I started, there were 2 training locations for Tai-Chi Jitsu...one was an old building located on the corner of Artesia Blvd. and Santa Fe Ave. in Compton, CA. The other location was the garage at his home on Poinsettia Ave. also in Compton. It was clear to me that Master Peterson was a very proud and disciplined man that gave respect and expected the same in return. With a background of over 2 decades of United States Navy military service that started during World War II you can imagine that discipline and respect were and are still part of his core beliefs. The other discipline came from having to fight, to defend himself against bullying as a youth on the streets of Milford, OH.

Myself and classmates in Tai-Chi Jitsu were challenged and pushed by Master Peterson to work hard and believe in his system of self defense which combined traditional elements of Oriental fighting arts with practical street defense. Many times I was encouraged to not add or take away from our system to this very day. The reality however is that martial artists worldwide borrow from each other. We learn a particular system but we are and should be flexible to learn something new if it helps and suits our individual abilities. Learning is not a finite practice. If one is open-minded learning becomes a life-long journey.

Tai-Chi Jitsu is a combination art that encompasses the bulk of Master Peterson's training through the years. He was good about allowing guest instructors to share with the class from time to time. He took us to tournaments and seminars to give us first-hand experiences as well. It is safe to say that Master Peterson did not play when it came to training. He did not run a social club. He was firm and did not allow unsolicited talking during class. In fact too much talking would have gotten you extra push-ups or an early dismissal from class.

If you attend a seminar given by him today you will quickly come to appreciate the importance of zip it, listen and learn. In other words, When the teacher is talking everyone else needs to listen. That is how he was taught and that is the way he teaches. I appreciate the fact that he pushed us. Those of us who trained under Master Peterson learned that discipline in the dojo also has led to discipline in life. Our training as it has turned out provided confidence, personal development, mental and physical strengths along with multiple other benefits.

Master Peterson is quite knowledgeable and skilled in the martial arts, leadership, showmanship and is a master storyteller which you will come to discover later. In fact, if you get the opportunity to sit down and talk with him he could share stories that span a portion of at least 10 different decades. We could literally write a separate history book on stories alone seen through his eyes over his years on earth. He has been very instrumental in promoting and participating in the martial arts in this country. From the East Coast to the West Coast and from the Southern Border to the Northern Border, Master Peterson has been a major part of the growth of martial arts in this country.

He has competed in, judged, instructed and promoted the Arts throughout his life. He has taught and officiated many students over the years including the military, kids, seniors, celebrities, law enforcement and many of the top boxers and martial artists in the country. He commands respect because of his undeniable leadership in teaching and sharing with generations of martial artists. He competed in and has won several competitions. He has been recognized with several hall of fame inductions and other major awards and still is actively demonstrating in seminars from coast to coast at the seasoned age of 96 years young which he reached on March 3, 2021.

Master Peterson is also a talented cook. Due to racial inequalities at that era in our country and the lack of opportunities for him upon enlistment, he was initially trained to be a cook. Cooking was one of his primary duties when he started in the United States Navy during WWII. I mention this because he would take time to train you, teach you about life and even feed you afterwards. Spaghetti, goulash, chili and anything barbecue were some of the meals that I remember he prepared well. Even today should you visit him at his home in Arizona, he will make sure that you eat well. His wife lovely Elida is a great cook and quintessential host. He still throws down in the kitchen from time to time to this day.

Fred Peterson was always concerned about his students outside of the dojo. Be it giving advice, trying to help one get a job, attending a wedding or other common life event, he was there. Those of us who attain certain ranks and titles in the martial arts know that wearing multiple hats come with the territory as the cliche goes. He wore many hats back in the day and was proud to do so. He stays ready to share martial arts experience and protocol because of his extensive knowledge, in other words "He's been there and done that". Mr. Peterson is extremely passionate about the preservation of history, respect and the traditions of the martial arts.

Now that I have transitioned to a more present tense in this narrative, I formally present to you Soke Dr. Professor Great-Grandmaster Frederick Douglas Peterson Jr. a.k.a."Big Cat." Why comes the name change? At the time when I first met him he was referred to as Master Peterson. Since October 1984 when I first met and began training under him much has occurred. The many accolades that occurred include rank promotions, awards, multiple hall of fame recognitions, appearances in publications, trophies, plaques, certificates and acknowledgements by several well-known grandmasters in the martial arts world. Over the course of three and a half decades I have learned and continue to tap into his vast reservoir of knowledge. Soke (head of the family) Fred Peterson enjoys what the martial arts have done for his life and he will share thoughts and experiences with you. The amazing observation that jumps out at one is that each time you sit and have a conversation with him it is likely you will get a different nugget and learn something new about a life-span that many will not get to experience. Soke has outlived most of his contemporaries and even many notable martial artists well his junior in age. Yet as he would say the almighty God has kept him here for a reason. Perhaps Soke is meant to be a bridge connecting martial arts generations from the 1940's until today.

Soke Peterson chose and promoted me to carry-on the Tai-Chi Jitsu System of Self Defense. I consider it an honor and privilege to keep the system alive. One day I will pass it over to another who will keep Soke Peterson's legacy alive and of those who poured into his life. We invite you to read on and learn about this living legend. He is upfront and candid about many of his life experiences. At his age some have said he has earned the right to tell it like it is and was. Some of his stories will surprise and some may even shock you. Yet, these are the words of a man whose life has spanned close to a century on earth. He loves to see that interest in the martial arts remain strong and considers himself like a father, grandfather and great grandfather to many who practice the Arts today. In addition to Soke Peterson and I, the third contributor is Dr. Danny Layne. He has insights that preceded my time and initial experiences with Soke Peterson. Dr. Danny Layne trained under Guru Danny Inosanto and Soke Fred Peterson concurrently. Danny Layne is a student of Soke's who also was a brown belt under Guru Danny Inosanto when he came to train with Soke Peterson. Dr. Layne compared many of Master Peterson's teachings to that of Guru (master) Inosanto's teachings and has been promoted to Dr. Professor Grandmaster along with inductions in some of the same hall of fames along with Soke Peterson over the years.

We hope many will find this autobiography to be eye-opening revealing and inspiring. Together, Soke Peterson, Dr. Layne and I will share with you the life experiences of the man nicknamed the "Big Cat." We believe this story will amaze, surprise and even humor you at times. It has long been said that a picture is worth a thousand words and we have pictures that will also help tell the narrative of this remarkable story. For the layperson there are words you will find in parentheses ( ). This was only done to help non-martial artists with the meanings of words that may not be common to your understanding unless you are a practitioner of the arts or have knowledge of certain military terms. We could have shared many more photos but there will be more if another edition comes about later.

One question that some readers may have is "how did this book project come about? I was amazed to find out that Frederick D. Peterson Jr. did not have a Wikipedia page. Despite all of the history witnessed and seen through his eyes there was not a page dedicated to the documentation of his amazing life. Many individuals who have lived a mere fraction of his life have pages. The original thought was to author a Wikipedia page but it led to the life story and journey that is now before you. My encouragement to all who have a special mentor in your life is to document and capture living history while you can.

Trust me when I say that this book could have easily been twice as long. There were many stories that could have been included but were not. Soke Fred Peterson is 96 years-old and to say the least there is a great deal to remember and recount but he did a phenomenal job. The majority of you who will read this book would probably have difficulty recalling half as much should you live to be his age. So we invite you to embark with us if you will on a journey that includes nearly a century of contact with historical figures, continental travel and many life experiences that can be referenced straight out of the history books. Get ready, it is time for Soke Frederick Peterson's story.

--Thomas Hardie 7th Dan, Tai-Chi Jitsu

THE LIFE JOURNEY
FROM THE ORPHAN TO THE SOKE
Frederick Peterson
(IN HIS OWN WORDS)

Chapter One

The Early Years

The life of this Soke Doctor Professor Great Grandmaster Frederick Douglas Peterson Jr. (Big Cat) started at the Grady Hospital, in Atlanta, GA on the second day of March 1925. Two other siblings were born at this same hospital to Frederick Douglas Peterson and Fannie Mae. The first sibling was named Robert Jerome who died at childbirth and the second was Frieda Mae, who is two years older than me.

It took sixteen years for me, Frederick D. Peterson Jr. to find out that all my life up to this time, I had only the name of Baby Peterson Jr. on my birth certificate at Grady Hospital of Atlanta, GA. When I had to contact the hospital to obtain my birth certificate so I could enter the United States Navy in the year of 1943 there was a delay. It took a few profane words in writing to the Grady Hospital who claimed they were waiting for proof from me as to the names of my mother and father.

Through the tradition of oral storytelling it was shared with me that I am the great, great, great grandson of Thomas Jefferson. Yes, the 3rd president of the United States is my great, great, great grandfather. I do not have any paper records to show for this. I only have what has been passed on through storytelling down through the line of my family.

[Editor's Note: *Thomas Jefferson (April 13, 1743 – July 4, 1826) was an American statesman, diplomat, lawyer, architect and philosopher. As a Founding Father of the U.S. Constitution he also served as the third president of the United States from 1801 to 1809. During his public service he served as a state governor, U.S. Secretary of State and served as a foreign minister as well. Like many of the founding fathers of this nation, Thomas Jefferson was also a slave owner who fathered amongst his slaves from which Frederick Douglas Peterson Jr. is in his unofficial lineage.]*

My mother Fannie passed away while I was still just a baby living downtown in Cincinnati, OH from the sickness of Strep throat. As a young father all three of my daughters would later suffer with the same infection but were cured by U.S. Navy doctors. My sister and I were accepted to live for a short period of time by our mother's cousin whom we called Aunt Tabitha. She lost the care of my sister and I due to her leaving us at home by ourselves one time too many. After we were placed in the care of the orphan home I was taken to somewhere in Kentucky to be raised by a doctor, his wife and their child. Only due to the begging insistence of my sister, Frieda Mae, whose name was changed to the name of a lady named Maude Jane Bennett in Milford, OH. did the orphan girl find me her brother and bring him to live with her in Milford, OH.

Fred and Maude Bennett soon had us two plus a few other orphan kids to care for. My sister and I went through fourteen years of our lives living with them, attending Milford Jr. High School. Not only did we attend the African

Methodist Episcopal Church on High Street but also participated in all of the services, singing, acting in plays, open professions, and not failing to sit no further back than the second row, if the first row was full. It is due to sitting on this first row in church that we went from getting our tails whipped for clowning in church and getting praised for joining the church and getting my tail tore up at home shortly after joining. Since the tall handsome evangelist gave all the pretty girls who went up to him a big hug, I followed my sister, reaching out for my hug, but getting held away from him by my bald head in his big hand while he called out to our foster cousin Gladys to take me and pray for me.

My tail whipping came later that same evening when I called myself doing a great Godly thing by confessing to Mother Bennett all of my past sins like sometimes stealing the loaf of bread at the store, buying only 10 cent worth of coal oil for cooking where it took 12 cent to fill the jug, asking a girl for a piece of her fine butt on a note in school, which I had told my Mother Bennett that I wanted the piece to put it in a jar of alcohol to save. As you can see my confessions back-fired because Mother Maude and my sister Freida Mae had to work hard doing laundry for the white folks in Milford OH.

There was hardly a day that went by that I did not have a street fight in Milford. As an orphan I always felt that other kids picked on me. I never respected size or age because I was not a clean fighter. I left my teeth print in one big bully's jaw when he threw me. He reminded me of this when we were grown and I visited home. He had not too long ago won the lottery and would not give me a penny.

My greatest love was sports. I could never play anything but sandlot (a vacant lot used by youngsters for games or sports)baseball and football because even though I was known to be a tough nut, I never weighed over 134 lbs. This was my boxing weight later in life. It was hard for me to find fights because I am a lefty. Many heavy weights trained with me before, during and after the three wars: World War II, Korea and Vietnam. They used the BS of punch control until we got used to each other. Of course I recall making a couple of heavy's take the gloves off in front of the ladies they wanted to impress because they couldn't hit me. I always, even as a kid considered that defense comes before offensive training. The reason for this is that fist and/or feet can do you no good when you are dazed or out on your feet. My being a lefty only comes into effect when I am fighting, pitching or throwing since I am right handed in every other necessity of my life.

All but one year of my youth education in school was performed in mixed schools of race, one year being performed in an all black school which was a repeat of the seventh grade at the Milford School. So much so that our math teacher, Mrs Dyer at Douglas School in Walnut Hills, OH, whom my sister and I lived with for a few years by the last name of Mrs.Henson who taught a lower grade. Mrs. Dyer actually had me teaching the first year Algebra course. Even while teaching the class I had a female classmate that was always throwing kisses to me. It was fun to teach.

Since I seem to be getting ahead here on the history of my life, let me go back to one of the things I remember happened to me in Kentucky. I was awake just in time as a youngster of about three or four years old, to observe a very bright light coming toward my face from just over the top of the door. I was so afraid as a kid that I buried my head under the cover. From that night on in my young years I got my butt spanked for being so skinny that my sister, Frieda and Mother Bennett thought I had gone out the window until my body movement was seen at the foot of the bed.

At about the age of five years old, my eight year old sister found this package under an upstairs bed that she had been begging the orphan home and Mother Bennett to please give to her and that was her little blue-green eyed only brother, whose eyes she spotted looking at her from under the bed, where he (me) was hiding. Many of my young years I feared the darkness in our house and would not go upstairs without turning lights on the steps and the rooms until I was going under the covers. Mother Bennett had a saying that I could never understand until one night the true meaning of which came to me when I was home on boot camp (U.S. Navy) vacation. The statement she would say to me was "you are alright with me but the folks upstairs are kicking about you". Mother Bennett and Daddy Fred were very religious parents and she was speaking of how I must please God in my life more than her and anyone else.

I like to think that I was a good student in my first seven years of school at Milford Junior High although I did fail in the seventh grade, the same as my sister and fought many days. One of the very prejudiced brothers whom I got even with during my vacation (what we call Leave in the U.S. Navy) having just returned from WWII in the South Pacific in the year of 1945 since this young white boy knocked me down when I made it safely to first base after getting a hit during recess. It seemed no one at the school did anything on behalf of our black children.

I crossed the street in downtown Milford, OH to address this same young man while accompanied by three White girls and immediately put an end to their joyful trip. I only spoke to him wearing my uniform and medals, decked(hit) him and was about to stomp him in the face when my friend shoved me back from him and hollered at me to run with him before the Milford cop saw us. We made it home and as I was passing by his brother's house on that Sunday morning having just attended mass at the catholic church there since I had converted to Catholicism upon marriage in the Philippines. He called me over to his porch and immediately thanked me for my service of knocking some sense into his oldest brother as he put it.

My sister Freida Mae, and I lived very good lives under the guidance of Mother and Dad Bennett with having three full meals three times a day, taught proper cleanliness and hygiene both inner and outer of body, taught how to keep clothing, house cleaning, and cooking for me at the age of six, while my sister and Mother Bennett supported the family financially by doing laundry for the white folks who could afford it.

I at times was the only kid, during the hot days of the summer time, observed hitting a ball up and down the field in front of our house until the cool evenings. That's when other kids joined us to play ball with whatever equipment we could put together and followed by playing hide and go seek. There were a few very nice looking young girls who played with us but I accepted only as only friends.

I don't recall when the news of our father Frederick Douglass Peterson's death came to us and neither did my sister and I remember being told that he served in World War I in Europe and contracted Tuberculosis. My dad died in Dayton, OH at the V.A.(Veteran's Administration) Hospital after having seen me one time without me knowing he was hiding behind the door at our real cousin's house, who was a dentist in Milford. He had me turn around and around for a while and then had me go downstairs to his wife to eat dinner. It was told to me that my father was looking at me from behind that door.

Chapter Two

Introduction to Boxing

When I returned from WWII and went home on leave, this same cousin took me to visit my Aunt Tabitha who I spoke of earlier in this letter, also a visit to a barber who served with my daddy and told me he had something that he wanted to give me before he died, which I never received. Prior to returning back to the Navy from this leave I also met and had a couple of good nights with two lovely ladies I had courted prior to going into the U.S. Navy. It was a day in 1943 that I decided to join the U.S. Navy in Cincinnati, OH. Prior to this decision I had been used as a punching bag during recess both by a good amateur boxer at Milford Junior High and also by a professional boxer who lasted two rounds with "Sugar" Ray Robinson as a middleweight.

A member of our gang in Walnut Hills, OH, who brought me into the gang after beating me down in the street near my house, asked to come over to our basement in the Henson house by him to make a boxer out of me. After several butt whippings I became rather good at defense, in fact, so good that I proved to give a very good lightweight in our gang. I was tough in a fight every time someone sparred with me. Later I started going to Withrow High School near Avondale, OH, known to be the fourth ranked high school in the United States. Well I took my Cross Country running and my training at boxing more serious than my subjects and ended up failing in the 11th grade. My English teacher who made this possible or at least gave me an excuse for the failure told me she would be waiting for me to come back the next year and I told her she would not see me again.

I joined the U.S. Navy after having the left-side of my nose operated on, so I could breathe through both nostrils properly, needless to say, this was a very painful operation. I never got to box in my hometown but I did train a few days at the same stable as a great professional heavyweight Ezzard, "The Black Cobra" Charles, Floyd Gibson, Newsboy Seal, David Clark (The middleweight I spoke about earlier) and Sam Birch (the lightweight) I spoke of. By me being a lefty and pretty good I spent many evenings on troop ships such as the President Jackson, going over to the war in the South Pacific, fighting in smokers (unsanctioned boxing matches held at military bases) and at Guadalcanal, Bougainville and Leyte in the Philippines.

My final boxing match was against a lightweight professional whom light heavyweight military champion Gus Lesnevich weighed me in for after requesting that I try this pro out to see if he was still any good after getting shot in the leg. The pro boxer won and I promised my girlfriend, Clemencia (Esing) Codia that I would never box again, which I have not. After retiring however I did teach some boxing skills from the Navy to Compton, CA.

I used the boxing experience to enable me to be a well-liked and respected referee, judge and timekeeper both as an amateur for the AAU (Amateur Athletic Union), later USA Boxing, Golden Gloves, Silver Gloves and five Olympic trials. At one of them I found that I had disqualified Hector Macho Camacho Jr. from the Olympics. Much later I received several hugs from this same former WBC (World Boxing Council) Champion when I served at several Indian casinos in Southern California as a professional timekeeper for over 38 years from 1976 to 2014.

Chapter Three

Return to My Childhood

Permit me to go back to my childhood after the orphan home system of Cincinnati, OH moved me into the home of Maude Bennett of Milford, OH to be joined up with my sister, Freida Mae Peterson. I believe her name was later changed to Maude Jane Bennett as mine was changed to Fred Bennett. Milford is a very small little country town in Ohio where everyone knew each other even though most tried to avoid each other especially if you were of a different color.

We played ball with any equipment we could get our hands on. I believe I took part in one track meet while there also. The only other activity I can remember during my young days there in the evenings we went to church where my sister and I had to either sing or say a speech, participate in all of the plays and I sang "Swing Low Sweet Chariot" in the Milford Auditorium, I got clapped back and the music teacher got mad at me because he told us not to perform again no matter how long they applauded. I was hard-headed and I sang again anyway.

My most favorite family memories were my trips every Friday to the big farm of Mother Bennett's parents and Aunt Betty who was a lady to really be admired. Daily she would jump up in her buggy which was pulled by the smartest horse on earth named Doc. He would take her to a different White family's house each day and go through town to the barn of Mr. Jackson. Now after being fed and brushed down he returned to where Aunt Betty was working that day, and he would eat the people's grass while he awaited her to get into the buggy.

On cold snowy or rainy winter days Aunt Betty would put the big black canvas down around her and tell Doc "go get Fred". She could not see where he would go, but he would go through town to our house stop in the alley. I would run out of the house, jump up in the buggy, pull the canvas back down and sometimes tell Doc to go home, which he would go five more miles and make three stops if necessary, one at the red light, the second to make a left turn to go up the hill and the third, to stop behind the house up on the farm.

Aunt Betty would take him to the barn, feed him, and the other animals, perform other farming jobs with my help. Help my foster grandmother to care for my granddad, who was blind, check on the bathtub beer, which would be emptied so we could take our Saturday night bath, getting ready for Sunday service. The main routine I hated was the inside body cleaning at home every Saturday night which was your choice of Black Draught, Castor Oil or what we thought was chocolate candy but learned different when my sister and I stole a bar of Ex-Lax and the druggist let us know that he saw us but wouldn't stop us. We ate it on the way home, and a man stopped our running home to ask us the way to the same drug store. We continued our run and hollered back at him to just follow the yellow streak.

On most Saturday evening's we would go to another of my loves, along with most families in Milford and that was the little park ball diamond along the river. I loved to be either the softball lefty pitcher or left fielder. Occasionally I would get a chance to pee my pants from laughing so hard at the Jackass Softball Game. Don't miss going to see this type of ball game if you ever get the chance and take a towel to cover your nose especially because these donkey's talk out of the wrong end a lot during the game while they buck up and down.

My foster father, Daddy Fred Bennett was a barber and we believe that smelling all of this hair products many have got to his system and caused his death. He actually died twice because I went to school one day after the doctor pronounced him dead and they had to pull Mother Bennett out from under his bed. I didn't want to leave but she told me to go ahead and that daddy would be alright when I came home. It was true because he was sitting up in bed smiling at me when I got home. Dad Bennett like his sister Mary had the sweetest voice for singing I have ever heard. A short time after this he did die and I was very hurt.

Shortly after this my sister was moved to Walnut Hills to live with the Henson family. He was a retired realtor and she was a schoolteacher. I found out again that it was a big nice house because Mother Bennett went to Florida to work for this white family and I would not tolerate my Aunt Alice raising me.

I prayed many times for my Aunt Alice, who stayed for a time with her sister Mother Bennett. She was from Chicago and a great seamstress. A beautiful woman with a lovely body and loved the night life in bars where if a man touched her he might not have a hand to touch anyone else. She got great respect.

Mother Bennett died from Alzheimer's disease and all this was after I had come back from WWII and was so sad to see how she could not remember who my wife, Clemencia (Esing) Peterson was even when they were sitting there talking to each other and Mother asking over and over about "How is Rosey" who is my baby daughter and whom she loved so much.

Aunt Alice was talking to me one day after the Memorial Day Parade which I took mother to in a wheelchair, and one day Mother Bennett called her next door to her house to tell her that she called the police because a man had broken into her bedroom. Aunt Alice said she told her that she wished a man would break in her bedroom window and how she would take care later of anyone who had called the police. She also told me that she had made arrangements with the only two undertakers in Milford about what to do with her body at her funeral. She said they were to place her naked, on her stomach in her coffin and the coffin was to be opened at the bottom so the people as they passed by could see her black rear end.

I did not go to her funeral. I have only visited Milford a couple of times since being raised up there. All of the foster families are gone on up above. I prayed for Uncle John, who loved to see me throw rocks as far as I could across the big field in front of our house as a kid. Uncle Frank who always made sure we had fresh water fish and plenty of vegetables which the stores were going to throw away and he was called the Black "Mayor of Milford." Later in my life I found out that you couldn't only purchase a pint or so of good whiskey from his house where Aunt Alice also lived for a while. It was a young lady, my first girlfriend in Eden Park of Walnut Hills, Ohio who took away my virginity on a school ground during one of my newspaper delivery routes at the age of fifteen years-old.

Chapter Four

From the Teens to the Navy

Now we come to my young adult years which were living with the Henson family, whose daughter had just married the owner of Renfro Funeral Home. After completing the one year at Douglas School, I went to Withrow High School which I spoke of earlier. During these years I had my share of street fights both personal and with our gang which controlled the Ashland Street Park on Walnut Hills where we did all of our out of school activities with our "A" scratched by a match stick on our arms. This got the others a good tail whipping if they were going to the movie with only the 50 cents it cost. The Cincinnati Gang would take your 50 cents and give you a beating for not having more. Never did they mess with me or my sister because she went with and married the best friend of Ezzard Charles who beat Joe Louis later for the heavyweight championship of the world. I later trained at the same stable as him but only for a short time during which I was around 15 yrs-old.

I had my own paper route of over 300 customers, performed any type of work to make some money like putting in coal which would be dumped on the sidewalk. My price was fifty cents a ton, which I would drag to your cellar door and dump in. Many times I would cause the grass I cut with my push lawn mower to turn brown because it was cut too short. Dr. and Mrs. Edwards always paid me 50 cent to a dollar for this or a dollar to wash with Spic and Span their kitchen walls. I kept a pocket full of money and brought my first long pants suit which I wore proudly to church for the first time.

My sister was accepted before she got married into what we called the sadity crowd of youngsters and they had their meetings and dances in their home. We as a gang were not ever invited but were very welcomed when we crashed the dances by going in through the windows. The bright lights would go out. The overseers of the sadity group were alerted but soon gave up because the girls loved our dance style.

I never accepted the girls as no more than friends when I had the urge but since I was an athlete I would only kiss them and move on if they wanted to go further. David Clark, my boxing teacher and gang leader I spoke of before always seem to follow behind me and misuse these hot young girls. One of the girls saw me one time on the bus and did not want to talk to me but was crying. I finally found out that she was mad at me because she got pregnant by David Clark and not me, no more could her mother call me to take her out. David married a girl I went to summer school with and visited a couple times too many because me and him met in her yard and we agreed to ask her right out who she wanted. She chose David. When I visited her house in my Navy Uniform after the war, and I was already married, although my wife and kid were still in the Philippine Islands she cried because David had left her with child and had moved, I believe to Washington, DC. She told me in front of her sister that she often wished she had chosen me.

At the age of fifteen years old my actual adult life began. This was when I had to go to work for this wonderful man, Mr. Henson, retired realtor, heavy politician, I don't recall whether Democrat or Republican, but he would pay me to pass out the leaflets. When his party was elected he smoked a big cigar, when they lost he smoked a stub or none at all. One summer day we were sitting on his front porch and he asked me for my decision once and for all because he would only make his decision once. He asked me to let him and his wife adopt me. I would go back to school and finish high school, he would pay my way through the medical college of my choice after I have become a professional boxer and tried to be the lightweight champion of the world, or I could move into a preacher's home where he had arranged that I paid rent there, get a job and be on my own since the Orphan Home had already regretfully put me out. My sister was already married and living with her husband Leslie Stallworth in Lockland, OH.

I chose to get my own job, pay my own rent and rent the room provided in the attic of the preacher, his wife, a professional basketball player and his wife and their baby who I helped babysit and he would pay me. I worked for a couple of years at the Belvedere Apartments in an area of Cincinnati that we were not allowed unless you worked there. When I speak of we I of course relate to the horrible segregation very much present in my home which we only encountered when we tried to step out of our solely Blacks area to work or shop.

Let me mention here that even as a kid I would never go across the Ohio Bridge into Kentucky for no reason. The police or rednecks would most certainly be waiting to greet you with a beating accompanied with name calling and remarks you did not deserve. Of course our gang had certain areas in Walnut Hills that is where the white kids got what was coming to them. Especially as I recall one event in the park we loved, Eden Park. The southern whites made us give up the swings and thought we had gone but when their girls came across the little bridge rejoicing our girls came from under and ran them down and gave them something to carry back home with them.

Of course those so-called brave white rebels got a worst-off gift. I recall one time David Clark rocked the stop sign with one of them several times while we administered to the others. The police could never catch us because we would be over several fences before they could get out and into their vehicles and sometimes I wondered if they really wanted to arrest us because they only would ask us not to start trouble when we went to our park again. Eden Park was an open place to lose your virginity under the evening sky. There were so many participants that you would just say excuse me and step over people.

Back to my working as a bell-hop at the Belvedere, besides cleaning the entrance area, delivering mail, operating the self operated elevator, for which I got a dollar every Friday from this lovely rich woman who learned that I had no parents. She would give me a dollar just to push the elevator and ride up to her floor. I also helped the doorman park cars which in the winter snow and ice. I along with others would occasionally bang a car with another, and just park it and call the owner and then the garage to come get it. Of course I used the rich people's bed to please some of their maids at times since they thought I was so cute. We got paid twenty-two dollars every two weeks and made very few tips. Of course we had to shoot a few dice to try to increase our own take home pay or borrow from the winners enough to make it to the next check. Sometimes I lost all my money and had to borrow from one of the fellas that I just lost to make it to next payday.

Back in those days you had to have a good recommendation letter from your former boss or you wouldn't be accepted for another job until WWII started. Times of course were very hard during the depression, but I made out real good with my job and my newspaper route after work. I kept some money so that when my female boss refused to give me Christmas off from work I quit.

Well the preacher did feel sorry for me but I moved to stay with my sister and her husband in Lockland, OH where they both had good jobs during wartime. One morning I grew tired of sitting around and depending on them so I went downtown Cincinnati to join the Marines at 16 years old. They told me right away that this was impossible so I went across the hall to the Navy and made it to the physical where they found I could only at times breathe through one side of my nose. This happened to me firstly by a girl who shoved my face down into the gravel road from the back before I learned much later how to do ukemis (falls) in my commando training and Judo. This same girl told me as grownups in Walnut Hills that she had always loved me but I was so bad and wanted her big rear-end sister rather than her. Her sister was older and more mature than we were.

The orphan home representatives learned of my troubles since they kept close check on me but would never either tell me of my real family in Southern Georgia and Alabama, and neither could they get any info on us. They told me that they had received permission to do one last thing for me and that was to get my nose operated on. I did, and it was told to me afterwards by my beautiful black married nurse, who gave me a sorrowful kiss every evening and morning because my nose covered a large part of my face and it was very painful.

Shortly after this without my nose being completely healed I went back to the Navy recruiting office and they accepted me, sent me across the street to get lunch before going home with my phony orders. That read on the outside envelope...Orders to Great Lakes, Illinois as a Seaman in the U.S. Navy. When I got home and opened my orders, well to my surprise the train ticket and all were to Norfolk, VA to be trained as a Mess Attendant, Unit K West, Unit X.

After four of the worst boot-camp training of sailors I think our Navy ever performed due to the outright refusal of our whole class to be made servants out of $50 a month. I believe we drilled about three times under our White Chief Palmer who seemed to have cared less, exercised one morning when this tall and short officer made us get out of bed and go out. We gambled, fought each other, told jokes and showed sympathy to the poor uneducated southern blacks, made them take a bath and talk hip talk.

Like one of my big friends from Nacogdoches, TX, who had never breathed fresh air until he left the farm following a mile from sea to cannot see everyday and did not know what dress shoes felt like. He could set a lit match to the bottom of his feet and feel nothing. Those of us who tried to bully these classmates we learned from or kicked their butts. One of my home boys would not stop bullying this big Texas friend of mine even though he begged him to let him alone. I happened to be close enough to grab him one day when I turned after hearing a glass break. It was the window two stories high and he was hanging on for dear life, while Nacadocha was crying and telling him that she didn't want to hit him but she wouldn't let him alone.

Most of our class liked me because I boxed in the smokers (unsanctioned boxing matches) even with my bad nose. One classmate from New York could not stand me, who was picked to be the Master-at-Arms of the class because he was tall and big. One day he was trying to make me clean the hallway again and was really talking about what he would do to me if I got smart with him. Before he could finish this threat I hit him an upper-cut that he had to grab the banister to keep from falling backwards down the steps.

On the train going to Norfolk the conductor was surprised that the shades were pulled down on our troop car when the train stopped in Lynchburg, VA. He wanted us to get off to stretch but we told him "hell no and leave us alone." We were allowed to go into Norfolk, where at that time, you were just trained to fight a war for our country.

This was to be our first liberty break in our uniforms from our boot camp in Norfolk. There were folks letting everyone know in a town that they had signs in their yard that read "Niggers and Dogs stay off of our grass." Of course we had to go to the back of the public vehicle, where one time I witnessed this white woman answering her son's questions. "Mother look at that man, he has a hat just like my daddy." The mother said " yes" to each statement as he described what the proud Black chief wore, but when he asked his mother what was this man, the mother said " a nigger", and there's the evidence of the fact we still have a long way to go. We spent our liberty not in the main street area of Norfolk but in the colored area of Norfolk named Church Street. Keep this street in mind because I will have a lot to say about it after the war was over and I served as Shore Patrol on it.

Mother Bennett had married again to a wonderful and funny good head chef of the largest hotel in Cincinnati, named Edward Bell. He was not only proud of me for being a sailor and veteran, but would not accept me as a cook because he said we waste too much of the parts of food that under a foreign name they made big money by serving. He was a really good dancer by moving his big head, which I believe he did in Akron, OH, where he was a boxer and jail attendant.

Everybody seemed to love him when we visited there. After a short boot camp leave to go home I received orders along with about eight of the other Norfolk Boot Camp, Northern Sailors and two North Carolina Sailors to go to Moffett Field, CA to be trained as stewards and cooks to take care of the U.S. Navy Doctors and Officers assigned to the servicemen who were wounded in the South Pacific during the war by the Japanese.

I believe this was intended by the controlling personnel of Norfolk Training Center to punish our unruly outfit but they actually did us a big favor. We only served on U.S. Navy vehicles that were being used for troop transport to the Southern Pacific Islands and then from one battleground to the next. We had the great privilege at the age of 17 and 18 to be trained heavily in warfare combat, shooting Springfield 03 rifles that kicked me in my right jaw 50 times in one day, Judo Jiu-Jitsu, Kempo, bayonet and knife techniques.

We got good liberty in San Jose, CA. Although more of the people there knew what service we belonged to because we wore a Navy white hat, Khaki shorts and pants, boom shoes (un-shined but brushed off). You would find me sitting near the bar waiting to go see one of the most beautiful girls I had ever seen named Peaches, whose Uncle took her to town after telling me to wait on the porch. I waited so late and never saw her again because I didn't know that the next morning we were shipping out on the President Jackson Civilian Ship with the First Marine Raiders.

Our hospital and supply outfit called Cub Nine and stopped to pick up the 75th and 88th I think Seabees at Alameda, CA. I had sleeping sickness for three days at sea. We bunked about three decks down where everything and everybody smelled like fish. The only fresh water we got in our canteen was for brushing our teeth and drinking. Of course we ate good and only had to serve coffee at night to the officers since they were served meals by the civilians.

Of course old sleeping-sickness me, only served coffee one time as I remembered. I was made to do that for the Captain of or our outfit. He was so understanding and forgiving as the ship rocked the wrong way, the coffee went right down his back and of course I ran back to the galley after seeing him jump up and holler and ran up the steps. Later in the evening he sent word for me to bring him another cup of coffee. And I could have been shot because he did not see me again until we arrived to set up camp on New Caledonia. He had seen me later in a boxing match on that ship in the evening after I got used to the living quarters.

He had a son whom he wanted to box in a wealthy area of I believe North Carolina and he had me work for him. I did such a good job for him that he called me over to his tent to serve coffee to one of the greatest admirals in the South Pacific War, Admiral Bill Halsey, whom he served together with in the U.S. Naval Academy. I observed " Bull " as I called him, since we could not call officer's by their ranks, because if we did the Japanese Snipers would know if they captured them. They would slap my captain upside his head in greeting and ask him when are you going to straighten up and make Admiral, which he did a short time later when he told me he hated to leave me on Bougainville Island.

He left his Marine-trained dog, which had three Purple Hearts, from attacks on the Japanese. The captain was so surprised when he came to his tent and saw me out back playing with Rex in his dog pen. I had to walk that dog every morning around the camp. He was not supposed to trust any dark colored person, so I bleached my skin. This same captain before he left, had saved me from two court-martials. One of them was for not shining his shoes to go to a party one evening because it rained all day. I was assigned to clean the black out of the crew's dining tent ovens for three days.

I was to miss seeing the nightly movie outdoors because of this but the Master-at-Arms in charge of me, put a wood box out in the jungle so I could go out there to sit and watch the movie... case done. The other time was when he was laughing real hard with the Executive Officer who was to take over the base and I had to go before him for knocking a white seaman on his butt for a word he called me, which the seaman tried to explain at mass to the Executive Officer that it was a word everyone called each other in New York.

After this officer tried to tell me that he got along fine with the negroes in the navy that worked for him on his plantation somewhere in Virginia. I cut him off by telling him that I would never work for him on his plantation and I would knock him on his rear-end if he called me out of my name, and he told me to get the hell out of there. This is the captain that one evening, late in the night that saved us few blacks who had just finished saving them from dying or going to prison. This was the only time during the whole war I served in the South Pacific theater that we came close to having to use any of our combat training and this was to line up with our loaded rifles across from the white guys tents who had the nerve to want to back up those of them who had hollered the N word at us as we walked to our tent.

The whole area between our tents was lit up as we faced off with each other. This captain called me over to his jeep and told me that if I would talk to my guys about going back into our tents he would see the white guys. This occurred on Guadalcanal where our fellows after serving the officers during the day could be assigned to stretcher bearer (a person who helps to carry the sick or injured on stretchers) and our tent was right next to the morgue as our one fox hole was.

I came close to losing my life on Guadalcanal where I spent the earlier days in the hospital tent with Dengue Fever (A mosquito-borne viral disease occurring in tropical and subtropical areas) alongside of many Merchants whose ships were destroyed by the Japanese Pilots using our codes to attack and to depart. Many times we have seen our own fighter planes shot off the air by our own Marines by mistake. When it was time to go from Guadalcanal to back up the Marine Raiders again with a hospital and supplies.

We were instructed in a very hateful manner by our supply officer to drive the loaded trucks off of the LST (Landing Ship Tank), which had dropped its ramp way out in the bay, not knowing whether the wheels would grip or not. I was the Gunner on the third truck off after the first truck was able to make it. This supply officer was yelling at us from the top of his voice with not too encouraging words. When we returned we learned that the Japanese had bombed the whole ramp off of the LST as we could see and the base that the Seabees (men who built bases, bulldozed and paved roadways in World War II) made there, was named after this supply officer who failed to run into the jungle for security.

I might mention that I have in my possession even now the video and the book that one of the Flyers of the Scout Planes that flew off of a dirt path on our base to spy on the Japanese encampments on the front line, wrote describing most of the self defense techniques we had learned from the Marine Raiders and observed being used by them. Especially one night when if it was not for their return one night after turning Bougainville over to the highly untrained black outfit of the Army, who were killed like fleas while we had dug in on the beachhead (a beach on an enemy's shore that an invading army takes and controls in order to prepare for the arrival of more soldiers and supplies) and lots of prayers used many of these techs, and I saw one Japanese Sniper shot five times out of a coconut tree before he hit the ground.

We were waiting for evacuation to be ordered, Admiral Halsey's fleet and I think Admiral Nimitz also surrounded that whole Island and I mean it rocked all night. Later you could touch a person right in front of you in the chow line wearing our Marine Greens and it would be a Japanese. I heard a cook got five years in prison for running out and cutting one of their throats not far in front of me one evening.

We had so many Japanese and Chinese women in our prison camp, whom we could talk to through the wires and they knew more about part of the U.S. than we did since lots of them worked on our railroads and truck farms (a farm where people grow vegetables that will be sold in markets) prior to the war. My captain of the base finally got orders to go to duty in Hawaii where I heard later that he did make admiral.

I did not have to work for this captain ever again from Virginia because five of us were sent over from the supply side of the base to the medical side where we really enjoyed working for the doctors. We played good softball every evening after our work and of course I fought on the Admiral-Army Boxing team as the lefty light-weight, whom everyone wanted to train with. Not knowing how to fight a lefty, they promised to take it easy with the punches but they would get carried away as they got use to my style. There was one middle-weight, who was a great agitator, would always aim for my nose. Well he finally was successful once and did not break it, but he refused to ever spar with me again.

It was on Bougainville that us few stewards, officers, and cooks never regretted that we were not part of the first Black Navy Seaman group serving as lookouts, repairing and stowing equipment in preparation for underway operations for they had the worst jobs to do like burning our outdoor toilet crap, putting lime in Tojo's (Military Police) helmets on a pipe that we urinated in. Doing clean up around the camp including the military dog's droppings.

A few of them would volunteer to come over and help us serve the doctors. We also got plenty of sick bay alcohol from the doctors who loved to come over and out bet us in gambling games. The five of us were transferred to the Philippine Islands. where I jumped ship to be with the beautiful girls and only got tuba (Filipino wine) and friendship the whole night along with losing my whole seabag of my clothes and many war souvenirs.The ship that took us to Guam, Samar was pulling off and my outfit was waiting to move out on the pier in the little Filipino boat of which a couple of us fools were being paddled back in. I went many days with only one thing to wear: my khaki outfit and muddy shoes. Never could get my supply department to get any gear back.

This was one time in my life I placed my full trust in my master God for he tells us not to worry about what we are to wear or eat because he takes care of even the birds of the air so how much more for us who are made in his image. This was the worst day or two I had seen in the South Pacific, the mud was thick, and no one seemed to pay any attention to my jump ship, one outfit, but not hungry but to laugh at me and the other one or two. It had been two years since we had seen a woman except for Mrs. Eleanor Roosevelt who visited us at Guadalcanal one day after flying in a Fighter Plane with one of the Tuskegee Airmen (a group of primarily African-American military pilots (fighter and bomber) and airmen who fought in

World War II.) She ate in the Officer's Mess Tent where I served and Mrs. Eleanor Roosevelt made it her business not to leave there until she came out in the galley and shook hands with all of the black meal preparers including me.

[Editor's Note: Courtesy of wikipedia, *Anna Eleanor Roosevelt (October 11, 1884 – November 7, 1962) was an American political figure, diplomat and activist. She served as the First Lady of the United States during her husband President Franklin D. Roosevelt's four terms in office, making her the longest-serving First Lady of the United States. Eleanor Roosevelt served as United States Delegate to the United Nations General Assembly from 1945 to 1952. She was a great advocate for women's roles in the workplace and was highly esteemed nationally and internationally. Mrs. Roosevelt also worked for the civil rights of African and Asian Americans which ultimately led to a friendship with one of Soke Peterson's foster mother's best friends, Dr. Mary Mcleod Bethune.]*

Mrs. Roosevelt was a real nice lady who befriended Mary McLeod Bethune who I used to be afraid of when she came to visit Mother Bell for Sunday dinner off and on. I later came to have great respect for her because she was a important educator who worked on Negro Affairs for President Franklin D. Roosevelt. She also has a school named after her called Bethune-Cookman College.

[Editor's Note: Courtesy of Wikipedia, *Mary Jane McLeod Bethune (July 10, 1875 – May 18, 1955) was an American educator, stateswoman, philanthropist, humanitarian, and civil rights activist. Mrs. Bethune founded the National Council for Negro Women in 1935 and resided as president or leader for a number of African American women's organizations including the National Association for Colored Women. She is best known by many for starting a private school for African-American students. The HBCU (Historical Black College & University) that bears her name is Bethune-Cookman University in Daytona Beach, Florida. She co-founded the UNCF (United Negro College Fund) which African American and minority students benefit from to this very day. The great woman who served as a presidential advisor and ate dinner many times in the home that Soke Fred Peterson was raised up in was someone he grew to love and respect.]*

I forgot to say that our Cub Nine occupied Bougainville on the invasion and stayed there until we had to drive on the wrong side of the road because the Australian took over. I loved the 190 proof Australian rum but it knocked me out for a whole night and half of the next day. It was a good thing we worked for the doctors, I must mention here one doctor named Dr. Keafer, who along with all of the specialists was a Bone Specialist. He would attempt to save all the human limbs he could but he got a letter one day and was crying outside when he had read that when the injured were shipped or flown to Guadalcanal they would just cut off these parts and send them to the U.S. after that I don't think he tried to save anymore parts.

Since the morgue was next to our tent we would go over and not only visit the dead but observe with our hands how they died. Of course we would question the doctors and corpsmen (an enlisted member of a military medical unit) in the evening activities. I looked in the head of one and was told that a stiff Seabee had died from one drink of wood alcohol (crude methanol made by distillation from wood). Sick bay alcohol is yes and wood alcohol was no.

Our captain's doctor would not permit any female nurses in our outfit so my wish of being able to care for them was gone. I did get a kiss on the jaw from a beautiful star who put on a show with Bob Hope one evening. It was a moonlight night and Tojo always let us have only about every fifteen minutes on a moonlight night. We had one of us who slept naked every night and would not go into the fox hole until one night Tojo dropped a bomb close to our camp thinking they had hit the far away airport, and his naked butt came head first over us down in the fox hole.

Chapter Five

Meet My Beloved Clemencia

Our duties were not needed at all in the Philippines for they had their own servants, the Filipino's, but they let us hang around long enough to get our full pay for the first time. Get good liberty in Tacloban, Leyte in 1944, where after some bad sexual sickness was cured with daily doses of penicillin and no liberty for a week, a good Christian friend of mine requested that I go with him into Tacloban to this restaurant, bar that only catered to Blacks and Filipinos, not many of them went. He told me to wait for him on Pebergoe Street and he would come get me because he had to go ahead and make sure if this lady was ready to meet me. She served but mostly sang, accompanied by my friend Polo, on his guitar.

I had gone into one of the Chinese stores and had consumed almost a whole bottle of strong shock tongue alcohol (strong enough to cause dehydration, numbness of tongue) so I was not feeling or seeing too good when this beautiful lady finished her song and came over to meet me. After the introduction I was asked by her if I knew the tune to this new song, she wanted to practice called "I Walk Alone." Of course my alcohol allowed me to give my best rendition of it and from then on I was accepted as her visitor twice a day until I acquired the written permission from the U.S.A. to marry this most lovely lady. And I didn't even know her real name even when I went with her father after our wedding night to the city hall to sign our wedding papers. She had me calling her Rosita Montebro when her real name was Clemencia Codia. It was a big laugh for my TaTa (father-in-law) NaNa (mother-in-law) and her beautiful sister (Deding).

45

A couple of times she would attend the fights (boxing) with me but I know she did not like it whether I won or lost. This judgement coming from a lady who served for the Japanese during the day and killed or saved some of the other guerrilla prisoners (Filipino served warriors) and who taught me the secret of real knife fighting, was accepted by me after I fought this pro I spoke of earlier. I did spar a few times after that but no more showmanship boxing.

While training for this big fight in the Philippines a young soldier came and sat by the ring and then asked me if I would spar with him. Of course I was very cocky from never having lost, being a lefty who got great respect for that boxer training to fight me and then backing out at fight time. This young soldier beat my behind and I was shocked. He turned out to be world-champion Henry Armstrong's sparring partner. He taught me about so many faults my proud butt had that I couldn't remember all of them but did allow me to put on such a good show with this pro that if my legs were not so weak from loving my future wife. I would have caught up with him and knocked him out in the second round. I could not catch his butt, and the third round he buckled my knees with a punch in a corner and the bell rang.

Since it was the last person in Cub Nine division leftover seas when WWII ended because I was allowed to stay in Tacloban, Leyte, sleep at night at my wife's home, to come back on a ship to the USA where all of the celebration was over and I was given not only a complete new outfit but asked to either ship over to the regular Navy or get out.

Since I am an orphan and now have a wife who was expecting a little sweet girl to be born soon to support. I enlisted into the regular U.S. Navy and only stayed out for two days as forced to do so before one of my reenlistments covering 21 years of service. This event was after serving on 10 Navy work ships, decommission of Battleship USS. New Jersey and four U.S. Navy Air Stations, which served two terms of six months in Kodiak Alaska and on two U.S. Naval Ice Breakers. One took us to the most Northern point of Greenland, Alert Greenland, after getting frozen in for three times, a week at a time and having this huge Polar Bear slap the bow of our ship, swimming along with a partner who joined it as far as the ship could be heard.

Serving on these ice breakers brings to my memory of how we played softball on the ice, viewed every size and shape of iceberg there could possibly be. Being attacked by a crazy eagle, staying at our Gun Tub assignment for at least an hour a day to please the captain only to observe our freezing butts. We were chipping down all of the staterooms and food supply holes and painting twice because the captain was upset at us. This captain, P.T. Kelly who operated the PT boat (short for patrol torpedo boat) in Guadalcanal with the late President Kennedy, welcomed back at least, six Petty Officers who had gone over the hill in Norfolk, VA returned to the ship to be punished by Captain Kelly, who gave each of them a bust to Seaman.

When we got to Alert, Greenland there were about 9 soldiers who rotated after one year of serving there, who came aboard and when we asked them what they wanted above all it was ice cream and we drank the brandy they refused. Having been separated from my wife and daughter a couple of days after our marriage and not being able to get orders back to the Philippines, since there were too many Filipino servicemen who wanted to go back home.

I really took off in practice of my martial arts training, ball playing and female chasing with my unit. Sometimes we spent three nights in a row going ashore after work, instead of getting our rest. Being stationed a long way from Seattle, WA and closer to Vancouver, Canada we spent every weekend in Vancouver, supplying the girls with the ten dollar-a-gallon liquor we purchased from the officer's bar. Many times between going there, those women would make sure we returned the next Saturday by giving each of us the five dollar train fare.

Other times I would visit my sister and her husband who had moved to Seattle, WA with her children. It might be observed by those who are reading this that I have not spoken of my blood family except for my sister and the cousin who was also my false family in Milford OH. Well there is an answer to this since me and my sister had no family as we knew of. We were left to make our growing life decisions and disciplines as we saw fit and of course that depended heavily on our prayers which we lifted up to our Lord and our foster parents. In many events of my life I have felt their presence.

The great day finally came when this wonderful commanding officer, a navy pilot, took great interest in either getting my wife and kid here with me or I getting me transferred back to the Philippines for duty. Washington finally sent me this order to be flown via Hawaii to the Philippines to Cavite Naval Air Base. When my plane arrived at the Manila Naval Base the captain of the base, who was later sent back to the U.S. as a psycho, inspected me along with his jeep driver, questioned, the U.S. Navy grey chief's uniform I was wearing and stated that I had to shine my shoes on the street. He took me in his office and showed me a picture of how he wanted his men on his base and ashore dressed or they went to his brig (a prison especially on a warship). The only way you get out, if you were sent in was to have your executive officer of the base or ship to come there and get you out. I got away with having all of my hair cut off and shining my shoes on the trunk. The only thing I hated about this mostly was that the last time my wife, her family and the neighborhood saw me was with rather long straight jet black hair, due to my using homemade Kork (made out of mash potatoes, lye and vaseline). If you left it on too long you either had a sore head or reddish color hair. This caused many of them to determine that I was a Mexican or Cuban. My eyes are also blue-green to this day. My wife and the rest of the family were surprised about my head when I returned although they did not maintain it.

My Ta Ta and his friend would make me drink all of the Tuba which I like so much along with Sakesan. In the evening when it was a little cooler I got introduced to Escrima-Kali stick fighting by getting struck many times as they laughed. Neither could they speak much English so I had to learn the defense of taking those sticks away from them and going to bed. Today I demonstrate many methods of defense against and control of the stick. Everybody to me knew how to strike with a weapon although, they taught me to slant my strikes more like a sword strike.

Since I was not Filipino, I was not allowed to work in the Officer's Mess which I did not care for because I loved the hard work with the Seabees which partly included and finally meant that I got to drive semi trucks all over Northern Philippines and army bases. My wife and lovely daughter, who could not understand a word I spoke at that time but got used to being in my arms, moved to Cavite, Tabon Kawit, and we set up housekeeping there with the nephew of the Mayor. There were two other Americans who married Filipinos and one was a deep sea diver making big money which he shared to set up an electric generator so we could all have free electricity. You still took showers by filling a tank with cold water and pulling a chain, flushed the toilet with a bucket of water ready and kept buckets of well water for drinking.

My second daughter, Cynthia was born here on a memorable day for me because I had just got a hit at Rizal Stadium where our Navy team played the Filipino team and the pitcher was the Japanese who struck out Babe Ruth. Just before I was number one to go up to bat I had caught a hot ground ball with my bare left hand and had a big red sore spot in my palm. The outfielder threw the ball between first and second base and the first baseman was slowly going to pick it up not knowing that I was tipping down the baseline right behind him. When he bent over to pick it up I took off and stole second base with a mean slide.

One of my neighbors ran to the bus announcing to me that I had another baby girl born. My wife was such a strong female she was sitting up on the floor mat bed with our baby girl in her arms nursing. We had a girl acting as maid for us and her sister was visiting.

The chief in charge of the Seabees workforce was so impressed by the quality and quantity of work I did which included operating some of the heavy duty equipment that he recognized that I have my rating changed from Steward to a Construction rating. This never happened before and finally my wife, two children and I were permitted to go to my country for permanent residence.

On the way, in Pearl Harbor, my wife had a serious pain around her heart and became very weak. The Naval doctor there diagnosed her as having her bra too tight. It was due to an emergency call I made at the hotel to a local San Francisco doctor that the true cause of her pain was something reoccurring that she had suffered with as a child and that was Rheumatic heart and a very serious case of it. He permitted me to move her to a home (rental) in Bremerton, WA. There where my beloved sister had arranged for me to rent, and loaned us money for a couple of months until my allotment would come through and the

U.S. Navy and Marine Corps loaned me money once to pay for nurse care for my daughter, clothing and food and when my U.S. Naval full pay was finally established and it was retroactive and I was in tall cotton (on easy street) except that my darling wife was in a special quiet hospital room in the Bremerton Naval Hospital.

The doctor told me that she had at the most three years to live, which turned out to be more than fifty years, suffering later with Asthma that made her very weak even though I had to force her to retire from her seamstress work at the Garment Factory in Los Angeles. Prior to our living in Compton and San Diego, CA.

Chapter Six

Other Service in the U. S. Navy

I was assigned to all of these 10 ships and about 2 of the naval air bases I mentioned previously. One of the Chief Radiomen in charge of Communications aboard the USS Protector and served as the Chief Inspector of all of the Radar Picket ships in Port. One of the First Class Radiomen in charge was very surprised he got a passing grade because of his prejudice. He refused to let my Radiomen go visit their families or liberty by taking over, as he was supposed to allow rotations and inspections. The prejudiced First Class Radioman was jealous of me because I passed over him in one year. My executive officer had to go over there and order him to do this. He had come into the Navy as a Radioman and did not like me having converted to First Class Radioman from First Class Steward and making Chief the following year. I had attended and finished Instruction and Leadership School in Norfolk, VA.

President Truman, he was the one that ended racism in the Navy. Before Truman we had what we called three loaves of bread. They were lines three white lines for first class and we couldn't wear the regular insignia of the first class or Chief, we couldn't wear that. You had a loaf of bread and a quarter moon and three stripes on your uniform. And you wore the chief uniform even though you were 3rd class Petty Officer, we couldn't hardly afford it.

I told about how a steward got caught up over in Canada dancing and he got ringing wet. He took off his coat and all he had was a front and cuffs (chuckle), and he had a tie around his neck cause he didn't have a back on his shirt nothing but a front. We couldn't afford the uniform we had to wear, the Chief's uniform with insignias that were not Petty Officer insignias. Truman ended prejudice in the military. He put an end to it and we could start wearing the regular uniform and be recognized as a Chief. President Truman made those changes around 1948. I think I was Bremerton, WA. at the time.

I almost got sent to Quantico Marine Base in Georgia to be trained as a permanent Shore Patrol and was transferred later to San Diego Naval, Boot Camp where I taught Radioman "A" and "B" School, with no Blacks and I was the only Black to teach there at the time.

Before I go off on my time of duty on the West Coast let me return to Norfolk, Boston, Brooklyn N.Y. and Rhode Island where I mentioned that I served on several ships out of these places. This was also my chance to meet personally some of my real relatives which began when I got a letter from my sister that she had revisited our real female cousin who lived in Nantucket, Rhode Island and I was operating out of Rhode Island. I contacted cousin Ruth and made arrangements to go see her on the Nantucket Ferry. When she opened her door to the same big gray house that the rich whites owned she was so grateful to see me in my Chief Radioman uniform and introduced me to the elderly Indian man who just stayed there with her and sat by the front door. She had a foster daughter who was Indian well-mannered young girl living with her also.

One day while I was helping her fix breakfast, she told one about how her former husband, Cousin Grant had been appointed to be the Captain of the Nantucket Rhode Island Whaling Fleet. For two years straight before he died, two different Massachusetts mayors would spend some weeks visiting at her house to get away from their families during the summer and how no one could get a work permit on that Island without her approval.

During the fall she would run them all off the island before the ferry boat got frozen in except she had a hard time getting rid of this one dude who told her that he just wanted to be where she was. Cousin Ruth told him that she was going to be there right now, and later she would be in Boothill. He had better be on that last ferry for he would be getting nothing there from her.

She went on to take me later and show me the largest hotel and restaurant on the island and told me that it was given to her by her white cousin, one of the Gibson girls, sister to my mother. She told me that if I would leave the navy and bring my family to her big house she would turn the restaurant and hotel over to me because I was the nephew of the owner who was deceased. I told my wife about this when she was raising our daughters in Portsmouth, VA and she told me that she would rather go back to the Philippines, so I gave all that up for her.

I got orders to go from the USS Protector to the U.S. Naval Training Center in San Diego, CA to teach Radioman "A" School. Prior to this I might mention that I sat Ship Shore Communications duty in Dam Neck, VA. during the latter part of winter, which was quite far from my home in Portsmouth, VA, so I stayed on the base until the weekends.

This base had every size snake hole one could see and they not only told me that in the Spring the snakes would not only be crawling along the long path we had to follow to the radio station but also would crawl into your bunk at night and bite you when you moved. The corpsmen had already begun to load up the needles and you could smell the venom all around the sick bay. I have all of the fear and respect for snakes any man can have so I went to the Radiomen Office and requested a transfer anywhere else.

The funny part of it all was that I was still wearing the U.S. Navy Steward Uniform.

The captain of the base held inspection of course but it was cut short and I never saw him again. The chief in charge told me that when the captain stood on the other side of my work bench and saw me sitting there receiving and sending Ship Shore messages, that he had had enough. Before I went to San Diego, which was my last naval duty station I was able to visit a couple of times driving to see my real relatives, Cousin Ruth's sister's nieces and grandchildren of Cousin Lester Mitchell, and was very proud to have one of the baby boys named after me Frederick Mitchell, who is still in charge of military electronics, I believe at an aircraft base in Georgia.

My wife, Esing, refused to leave Portsmouth, VA, because of her job, home and friends after fifteen years, so I just sweated it out with of course only one lady friend and her family until Esing informs me one night by phone just what I had felt would happen very soon in Portsmouth, VA. And that was because my middle daughter was pregnant by the same boy I had barred away from my home before I left because to me he was a smart talking clown.

Soon, I think the other two daughters got fed up and saw the handwriting on the wall, so she called me and said they would be coming out to San Diego by the scenic Greyhound bus route. Oh what a joyful day that was and I had put an end to my affair but did not give up my weekend trips to Tijuana, Mexico to the Agua Caliente Race Track. I made the great mistake of taking my wife over there without her having a green card and I almost had the kids to raise by myself. It took hours for me to make the Border Patrol understand that I really did not know she was not considered as an American citizen by marrying me and or marriage approval by Washington, D.C.

Oh yes, she not only got that green card but also her American citizenship after she spent thirteen years in the U.S. to visit her parents and sister. She had only been back home for two weeks when we got a telegram that her mother had fallen down the ladder up to the house and died. We had a nice house we rented in a city outside of San Diego. I believe it is called La Mesa, because my oldest daughter went to Mesa College which had the worst football team that San Diego had at the time.

In San Diego I practiced my judo training seriously under a Japanese instructor, who taught on the base and after being thrown constantly by every black belt who visited the dojo (school). I was finally invited to a Black Marine Sergeant judo expert's apartment in the Naval housing and showed me his library with several books on judo and mental training.

One day I was informed that I had orders awaiting me in the School Office to go to the Vietnam War. I went straight to the office and requested my retirement since I had served 21 years. While I was serving on my second U. S. Naval Ice Breaker I met this steward who worked for me and told me about this beautiful black controlled city in Southern California, named Compton and advised me that he would live there on his retirement from our Navy. I moved there with my wife, Clemencia (Esing) Codia, three daughters, Yolanda Fannie, Cynthia and Rose Mary, after serving as a teacher (Chief Radioman) of the Radioman "A" and "B" Schools from 1963 thru 1965 in the U.S. Naval Training Center, San Diego, CA.

Chapter Seven

More Navy and More Martial Arts

It was around 1943 that I was introduced to the world of pimps and prostitutes after I volunteered to be a sailor in our U.S. Navy. A lot of my small salary was spent on these women of San Francisco, CA, while being trained by the First Marine Raiders in hand to hand combat (Original Master James Mitose's Kempo and Jiu Jitsu/Jigoro Kano's Judo) at Moffett Field, near San Jose California in Cub 9 (Medical and Supply outfit) during WWII and of course boxing in the South Pacific.

It was on the President Jackson Troop Transport Ship that I slept for approximately three days and nights before I was forced to serve coffee at night to the Officers of Cub 9. While serving coffee to the Captain of his outfit I spilled the coffee down the back of his Captain, who forgave him and made him his personal Stewart mate when camp was set up in Guadalcanal.

I nearly died from a high fever, due to Dengue Fever while living surrounded by many Merchant Marines who were burnt up from the 3 ships that had been set afire by Japanese bombers who used our codes in order to bomb our ships and fly back over the mountains undamaged. It was during the service to this captain that I was observed by him, playing with the big beautiful Doberman Pinscher. The Marine fighting dogs. The captain hollered at me to freeze because this dog had 6 Purple Hearts for injuries and would attack dark complexion people by biting into throats. I also was very much admired by this captain for his semi-pro boxing victories he did as a lefty to any who would fight him on Bougainville and Philippine Islands at the scheduled Smokers. I would get six cans of hot beer for the winner and three for the loser. The captain even offered him to come to North Carolina and teach his son how to box after the war.

It was in Tacloban Leyte P.I. that I was weighed in by Gus Lesnevich, light heavyweight champ of the world and was his last boxing match due to his future wife's decision. While training for this fight and having sparred with a couple guys on his base. This soldier, who I observed outside the ring, asked me to spar with him. I did and got many mistakes corrected, and later he found out that this guy was one of boxing champ Henry Armstrong's sparring partners.

Shortly after returning to the U.S. I not only continued sparring in boxing but also started teaching any sailors who wanted to learn self defense back in 1947. I actually taught on Ice Breaker ships that were old Russian oil tankers that the Navy modified to be Ice breakers. This was done because these ships weighed as much as three destroyer ships. They were really heavy and unstable on the open water you so much so that you would be doing good just to stand up. The ships would rock and roll as soon as they were untied from the dock. Food would come out of the ovens. The officers were chained to their tables. As a steward I would be rolling around trying to get their food to the table without dropping it or spilling it on them. It was a terrible duty, believe me. The ship was not stable unless it was breaking through the icy waters.

We made a gym out of the bottom level in these ships and that is where I taught self defense at. Most people don't know this but I also taught Savate (French form of kickboxing) for awhile. I served throughout the different U.S. Naval Stations of assignment and later on different ships like ten out of Norfolk, VA., Boston, MA. and Providence, RI.

I served as Shore Patrol in Jacksonville, FL. and Norfolk, VA. I also served as a Prisoner Chaser from parts of Virginia and Kentucky along with a number of European countries. Having once sat down with Lucky Luciano and his bodyguards during daylight hours one day. Lucky had to go to his villa before nightfall. My main duty station was in Portsmouth, VA. where my three daughters were raised.

It was during one of these trips, when the Greyhound bus stopped at a restaurant in Dam Neck, VA for the rest stop, where a waitress refused to serve me, Chaser Peterson in my official uniform and told me that I had to go to a back room to eat. I had the three prisoners sitting at the table with me. They were not asked to go to the back to eat. Of course when I lifted the flap on the case of my .45 caliber hanging on my side, looking at her and around to the manager he told her to serve me and shut up. Being refused service like that at restaurants was not uncommon at that time.

One nervous moment I had while stationed in Norfolk, President Kennedy came to visit the Naval Base. He was headed over to shake hands and I had my hand over the area of my uniform that was missing a button. It looked like I was actually saluting him from my heart (chuckle). I was covering that missing button but he didn't even come over to me. He just waved over there at us and walked on by and I was glad at that. I thought he was going to shake hands with everybody. He just shook hands with the chief that was on the end.

That was a gold button on my chief's uniform. I was supposed to be standing at attention and that is just straight up. But instead I had one arm down and one hand covering that button (chuckle). It was the one up near my heart. It looked like I was saluting from my heart you know like you do with the flag when you don't have a hat on. He didn't even come over there. He just looked over at us and waved and walked on by. I was glad of that. I was Chief Radioman at the time.

This and many other reasons gave me who was a Chief Radioman by now, great joy when I got orders to go to San Diego, CA. Naval Recruiting Base, to teach Radioman "A" School. My wife refused to go and take our three daughters because of her job and friends there in Portsmouth, VA, but she changed her mind before I retired there after having taught a couple of radiomen. In San Diego CA, Radioman "A & B" School classes, I as Chief Peterson was assigned to teach math as high as Trigonometry and the subject of Oscillators, which is the basic element of a transmitter in electronics. When this shore duty was at an end I was told by the front office that I was not only to be promoted after having passed the test for higher ranking of Chief, but I was also to be transferred to the war zone in Vietnam. Of course by this time I had enough of war so I requested and got my retirement after over 21 years of service.

Do in part to my military service I have traveled to and from many of God's countries throughout the world many times. I traveled to countries like the Philippines, Japan, different parts of France, six or more times, Italy, such as Naples and Rome several times. I was blessed by two Popes, Pope Pius the XII, and Pope John the XXIII, and escorted as a Fourth Degree Knight of Columbus, and Pope John Paul II in Los Angeles. I also visited Algeria, Casablanca, Spain (Barcelona, Valencia, Madrid), Crete, Norway, Turkey, Fatima, and Medjugorje and escorted Mother Theresa in San Pedro, CA. I visited Israel, (Jerusalem, Bethlehem, Nazareth), Virgin Islands (St. Croix) Mexico, Cuba (Guantanamo Bay) Bermuda,

England(London, Portsmouth), Guam, and across the U.S.A. over twenty times.

Many of the students that I taught my Tai-Chi Jitsu style of self defense to occurred while working full-time for the City of Los Angeles as one of only three Communications Electricians of color, are still to this date living in and around Compton, CA. Some students hold ranks up to master and grandmaster.

Grandmaster Thomas Hardie who I met at an exercise gym in Long Beach, has proudly accepted the teaching of Tai-Chi Jitsu in Southern California along with Grandmaster Gustavo Martinez. Some of the senior black belts in the system include Master Dunimus Nickelberry (formerly Willie Elam), the late Master Ricky Green, Robert Williams and Peter Feeney. Two or three others to be named are the Towel brothers, John and Richard, one of their wives who had her own students, Henry Wilson (deaf), Dr. Professor Grandmaster Danny Layne and the late Grandmaster Big John Robertson. I have promoted many black belts overall over the years.

Yes, I will now go back to the many changes that happened in Compton and as I told you before Compton was a most beautiful city, it was told to me before I moved there by many different people, sailors that I knew some civilians that I met, in my military service. So that's the reason I retired and moved to Compton, and as I told you I took great interest in continuing my officiating and also teaching of the martial arts. Now for two years out of about forty years I trained in the style of Gung Fu after already having been in Judo and Jiu Jitsu for 38 years.

For two years I trained at the school that was at Wilson Park in Gung Fu. I started out training under Master Hugh McDonald but he only did his sword thing and very little teaching but he used me mostly as a guinea pig for the fighting in sparring with the other students and what not.

Now in one bout I got my knee popped and I had to get it operated on because I caught the kick from one of the hispanic fighters he was a big fellow. He kicked in such a way that he lost his balance and fell on my knee. I continued to go to the class anyhow and I was seated out and with this big cast on my leg and Master Hugh Macdonald. He didn't notice that and when he got ready to test the guys for blue belts. He didn't want to give me the test he said "because you weren't trained and all you're doing is just sitting and watching". And I said " well it is all registered up here give me the test and see if I fail sir please", and so he did and I passed with flying colors. The fact is that I actually did better than most of the students that he had in the class healthy.

So he left to train as I understood Muhammad Ali when he fought Sonny Liston and that trick punch that the people all said it couldn't have happened how Ali knocked him out so fast but one punch you see that was a martial arts punch I think I always said that Hugh Macdonald was the one that taught him that.

Okay, so after he never came back I finally heard that a gentleman by the name of Master James Sharp was teaching there, and so I went and trained under him. And he had some very good other students in fact he had some good female students also they were tough. I was old. I had just retired from the service and I am about 47 yrs old so I am the oldest one in the class. But I don't think that Master James Sharp ever knew neither did Hugh Macdonald know that I already had 30 years of judo and Jiu Jitsu from the World War II which was "kill or be killed," another type of self defense so when he took a great interest in me because I did real good.

Finally when I finished with him because ah to tell you the truth, he would teach us but then some of the other ranking brown belts would finish the teaching because he was heavy on that marijuana. And he would go to the barbershop and come back when the class was all over because he had already taught these brown belts and leave it up to them.

I started sparring in the tournaments there and I would win every time I fought, and then I do recall one of the students came from down in North Hollywood, from Bruce Lee's studio and he thought he was real tough. So of course Master Sharp put me on him so he would go into all these flips and all these fancy movements and what not, and I would stand there and look at him so he finally got a good punch in on me. And then he threw a roundhouse kick and the next thing you know he was up in the air not flying on his own because I had thrown him with a judo throw. That is when Master Sharp called me behind the stage, and he talked to me and I told him that I had been in Judo over 30 years although I am still white belt.

I left him and I started teaching. In fact, he let me go back to when I had my knee in a cast. I started writing all of my instructions down that I remembered in Jiu Jitsu and judo. My Jiu Jitsu comes from the Jigaro Kano style and my Kempo is the original Kempo. It comes from Grandmaster James Mitose in Hawaii. And I didn't train under Master Mitose directly, that I had to tell one of his guys that did, his name was Bruce Juchnik at a tournament once. But he was very respectful and I told him "I said I didn't say I trained under Master Mitose directly. I trained under the First Marine Raiders who he had trained in it at Moffett Field in CA." which I had mentioned before. But after I started teaching and that was at the new Salvation Army that they made in Compton.

I started getting a lot of good students and they seemed to love my style. There were all types of races of people, Samoans, Blacks, Whites, and I had one white student and his name was Peter Feeney and he came to me through my priest at the church who asked me would I teach him and said he's an orphan under him and I said "why did you ask me will I teach him?" and he said "because he is White," and I said "that doesn't mean anything to me Father. I will teach anybody." Peter joined in and made a wonderful student.

So I continued teaching and said, "Well I'll teach at the Salvation Army," but I had to stop teaching there because of the bad kids. They would turn the light switch off which was just outside the door. And even before I could start teaching I had to move furniture and stuff all around because they had the place full of furniture. I had to move it outside and then move it back in. It was really a problem then with the kids switching my light switch on and off. The directors wouldn't do anything about it. They said "this is their Salvation Army gym," so you're just using one of the rooms here." I didn't have to pay for the room so I quit.

Later I moved and told all of my students that if you want to continue with me I am going to rent a building down on Compton Boulevard just across the street from White Street which ended at Compton Blvd. A bar was right across the street from there. Well I got some good students there. And I taught there for at least about 4 or 5 years. We had a bar in there and we had a kitchen, we had everything you could name. And then we would have a fish fry on Fridays and I will never forget that. And then we had a car wash to make money. I had a preacher that came around to help out. This church was raising money for me and all. And then I had my good students and I had two of the students. They were Hispanic guys and if one didn't come the other wouldn't come. They were with the Thunderbirds, the roller skating derby. They were tough and they loved my training.

I had a guy come to me and asked me if I would teach him and said that he had just trained with the great Filipino martial artist Danny Inosanto and he was brown belt under him and he had learned about Jiu Jitsu and judo but he wanted to gain more knowledge in it from me and so I told him sure I will. That person ended up being higher ranked than I was because he taught in Hawaii. He came back and his brother is still over there until this day. He is Grandmaster Danny Layne who lives in Carson right now. He is up there in rank. I am one of the highest ranking in the United States but he also ranks pretty high. Many masters over there appreciated the training he had gotten from me and Danny Inosanto. They ranked him real high.

When I started teaching in this school down on Compton Blvd., 6 guys walked in and I always insisted that anybody come in that they sit down. I asked politely and if they didn't then I would turn somebody on them. They refused to sit down and I asked, "Who are you?"

"You don't know us," one guy responded. "We are the Crips."

"Fine," I said. "Just wait one minute." So I stood with my back to the wall and I told them to line up and they lined up horizontally. And I said no... one behind the other, so they did. They said what is all this for and I said "well okay I want each one of you to hit me in the stomach 2 times each as hard as you can." Two of them did but the third one came up and said "I am not going to do it, I am not going to do it." Then they started to walk out and I said "wait a minute no no no you are not going now." I said "I request equal time," and they said "what are you talking about," you know real smart. I told them I said "line up across horizontal now like a sergeant do and put your back up against the wall." And they said "what for?" and so I said "because I am going to hit each one of you 1 time in the stomach," and they said "aww naw man" and I said "well don't come back here no more and mess with me." I bring all that up because Willie Elam, I don't know he had told his stepfather and his real mother that he was coming and training with me at my dojo. They would call me because I had met them and his father, who we called Pappa, was something like that. He was a real nice guy. I did not want to hurt his feelings. I said Yeah Willie is here, he is doing fine. Well I would look out the window and Willie would be going down the street with the gang and he never would come into the dojo. But one day finally I was teaching the class and something happened and I had to take a break and I walked to the window and there he was standing outside. I said "Oh Willie is coming in," and it took him hours to get into the dojo. And I was just about to finish and he came in and from then on I could not get rid of him. Today he is one of my senior masters, he drives a semi-truck, he is a preacher, and I am so proud of him. He used to talk with my wife Clemencia Peterson and she was from the Philippines, and he loved to talk to her. He would sit beside her bed when she was sick with rheumatic coughing, asthma and I had to break him away from her. And then he would always try to correct me in my conduct, and sometimes my conduct wasn't too good and I didn't mind it you know.

You know one thing I would never allow in my school was talking. I did not allow the students to say anything when I was teaching. I would tell them this one phrase and that was "lock it". Keep your eyes and your ears open and your brain open and keep your mouth shut. Do not say you cannot do this and all that kind of stuff. Do not ask me any questions until the end of the class. So my daughter came and brought a couple of her friends at one time. You know it is really something for a teacher to turn his daughter away. But they would not obey. They would run their mouth, they would laugh and carry on and I said I told you all to lock it and they would not do it, so I kicked them out. My daughter today tells me she is sorry that I did not keep her because she would not have had all of the kids that she has now and the problems.

I was in my office one day and I want to share about one of my students. I had a little Mexican Kid, he was tough. I used to go and help Kid Jason, the one they call "Coach", I used to help him every time he had a tournament which was about every 2 weeks. He would always honor me with a trophy. I did not appreciate nobody giving me nothing because I felt like I could earn what I wanted but I accepted it and that appreciation. And there was this little kid he would fight his tail off, I mean he was good. He would always do whatever he could do to make a point that is what he did. He kicked this kid in the back and the judges told him he was rough and you kicked him in the back. The kid said "I didn't kick him in the back, I didn't kick him in the back." Master Peterson, did I kick him in the back?" And I said "yes you did and don't do it anymore." So they let it go and did not disqualify and he won again. He just kept winning.

I had told the whole class that if anybody came into the dojo and say anything about me or want to join the school, come and tell me. Well this same kid who was the accomplished fighter came flying into my office that day and said," there is a great big black guy out here" and said "he is big Master Peterson" and he said "he wants to check you out." And I said "he wants to know what?" and he said "he wants to check you out." I said "oh okay go back out and train." So I walked out and I stood in the middle of the tatami (Japanese term for mat) and I said "who in here wants to check me out and I don't see anybody." And out from behind the door comes this great big black guy like he said. His name happened to be Big John Robertson and he told me he said "I trained under Sensei Steve Muhammad," and I asked him, well he was Steve Sanders before he changed his name to Muhammad. And so I asked him "why are you coming to me?" He said "well like I said I want to check you out." I said "you want to check me out then come onto the mat." "Come onto the tatami." He said "what is a tatami?" I said "it is a mat where I am standing. He said,"what for?" I said, "you said you want to check me out," and he said, "naw I mean I want you to teach me. I said " Oh, well come in my office then," you know and I took him back and signed him in you know and told him how much it cost and everything. He was very glad to do that and he said, "I came to you because I want to learn judo and jiu jitsu, and I said " well I don't know if you ever seen me at Sensei Steve Sanders dojo but I did go to it at one time, and I think you had a student in there named Mad Dog or Mad something like that," and I said " he had come to my dojo and I also have an assistant here named Sensei Gomes and he had challenged Sensei Gomes and I know he was a pretty good fighter you know when it comes to point contact so I didn't let him fight my assistant." And he said "well show me some of what you know," and the next thing you know he was going all over the floor.

When I went by Sensei Steve Sanders dojo he jumped up out of his chair when I walked in the door and he said "hold everything, hold everything wait a minute this fool done come down here you know and so he said "pay attention and have a seat" and so I did. And he sat back down and then he told me after they finished sparring and all I saw them doing was sparring with each other. And so he told them he said "this guy here is crazy he is throwing people everywhere, and he said "you're liable to get hurt. And so I told him that I did go down there and I didn't remember seeing you. He said "no I must not have been there that day.

In the very first class I had after that Big John showed up and I was teaching that same day the kids how to fall and he was practicing his first fall and even after I teach certain falls I would teach the tachi waza (throwing technique) that goes along with that. And I called him up to do the demonstration with me. And he said " do you want me?" and I said " yes you know how to fall now and I want you to do your best," and the next thing you know he's flying through the air, the Ogoshi the hip throw and so he went up in the air over my head and like a ton of bricks he hit the mat and bounced, and from that day on I never had any problems out of his ego and he'd say "that's what I'm here for" he said " I'm ready to learn. And Big John would question me, he'd say "what if I do this?' I would say "do it" and he charged at me with his head down, like they do in wrestling and whatnot. And he started rolling all the way across the front side of the front door, and I said " why don't you unlock the door and roll out" and he would get up rubbing himself laughing and then later on he would challenge me about something else. But, when he got ready to make Shodan (1st degree black belt) I couldn't just make him Shodan. I had to make him Nidan (2nd degree black belt) because he was such a good student. He knew he loved Tai Otoshi (body drop throw). You mention that to him and oh he has a big smile and he loves Tai Otoshi.

I had a lady and she used to go to the bar and come in one day and her name was Gladys and she wore these boots and ah the half boots and always dressed sharp and was built nicely. And she came to me to learn and she was about fifty years old. And I asked her one day I said "why are you taking martial arts as self defense?" and she said "I want self defense because I go to the bar all the time and I don't want them clowns over there messing with me" and she was from Texas, and she talked fast.

One day it was on a Monday I'll never forget it. The guy that owns the grocery store down the street he came over to the dojo and said, "Can I talk to you Master Peterson?"

"Yeah."

"Are you training animals down here?" he asked.

I said "Why do you say that?"

He said, "That woman Saturday...she went in this phone booth and I saw the guy when he went in there on her, and I don't know what he was trying to do but it looked like he was trying to get a little something.

"She put her back upside the telephone booth" he continued, "and she kicked him first."

He didn't tell me where she kicked him, and then he said, "The next thing you know he was rolling out in the street. She went and jumped on him, straddled him and was choking him, I mean she was choking that fool. It took three men to take her off and I thought I would come to tell you about it."

So, when she came to class that evening, I questioned her about it and she said "yeah, you told me to never let nobody get behind my back and always put a back up against a tree a wall or something never let them get behind my back, and then we can take care of them in the front. And I said " okay that's good that's good I like that," and she said "also I kicked him in his grand," and I said "grand, and she said "yes grand" I said " groin" and she said "you teach me martial arts you don't teach me no english I said grand," and so I just let let it go.

So getting to all of my students I had wonderful students except for one and there is always a show off in town and that guy he used to do flying kicks, spinning heel kicks, jumping spinning heel kick, jumping side thrust and I wondered why he always practiced it so much and then I would see him sometimes when driving down Compton, and he was out there jogging five miles and all that. One day he told me that he wanted to spar with me and Sensei Gomes said oh oh I'm going to officiate, and he said "okay", and I said "alright", and so he flew in the air and I went in a Judo roll underneath him and my feet just barely missed his groin. He's up in the air ooh ooh and he lands on the other side and then he figured that I was too old I guess to be able to catch when he come back with another flying side thrust and when he came with that one I was on my knees reaching up after his groin and he was hollering again and he said "okay okay okay" and I never saw him again, never saw him again.

I taught there for many years about three or four years and like I said we had good times. In fact on Saturdays and Sundays we had the dancing floor to make money oh yeah the people of Compton would come and it was a big hall. I had a bar. I had the pool table and everything. So there was the kitchen and everything and they would have their affairs and I did real good with that school. And finally the owner told me that he was renting it out to a Jewish man for a furniture store, and I had to move.

So, I moved to a big building on Compton Boulevard that had been a big garage or something I don't know why that building had big holes in the floor (chuckle) but I taught there and I believe that's where sensei who's a grandmaster under me now Tom Hardie came to me and it was a big building, and I would give tournaments there too but the Jehovah Witnesses did not like the noise as they told the police, and I was warned one evening by five policemen but the thing about it was the Black sergeant in Compton his son's, two of his son's were my students. And so I went on to work after I broke up the tournament because the five police told me they were going to write a charge up against me, and I went on to work and that Monday when I came home that evening the sergeant came to my house and he told me don't worry about it, it's all dropped, and I said "Thank you very much (chuckle)."

There I had a lot of good students join over there too, ah Tom Hardie I met him at one of the training centers there where weight lifting and all, and I noticed this nice looking young man, and he looked kind of healthy and muscular, and I said "why won't you take self defense martial arts and he said "I would like to" and I said "come to me," and I told him where it was and he came and I can't get rid of him today (chuckle) you know. He's a very great student, and at my age I turned my style over to him while I'm still alive. I think I'm the only high ranking grandmaster that ever turned his style over to a student before he died. The student can take over while the leader lives to eliminate confusion after the leader is gone on.

I had a lot of problems there with the people on that street and so I said "Well I'm going to give this up "I'm going to move out of here" I found another school on Alondra in Compton, and I started teaching there. It was an old cheese factory. The guy let me have it real reasonable and there I picked up a Mexican kid who was real good and Peter Feeney and he's still training with me, but one of the little black students didn't like him because he was white, and I could never stand that type of prejudice. And I went outside and he was calling Peter all kinds of names. So I called him in my office and I sit him down and I asked him why he was doing that and he said "because he was White, and this and that, and I don't care about him," and I said "well you can't be doing nothing like that, and he's trying to help you."

Peter was a brown belt and he was a real good in learning, and very muscular and very nice personality. And so I told him I said "he's only trying to help. I want my students to help each other and you hear me telling you that," and so Peter said "that's all I'm trying to do Master Peterson, and if he don't like me I'm still going to try to get it on." And I said "no you're not." I said "you go on ahead out," and when he left I just asked the kid out right I said "what is your problem?"

I said "the man has done nothing but try to be good to you and show you love and why do you act the way you do?" And he said Master Peterson I have a problem and I said "what is it?" and he said "my brother at night tells me and brag all the time at night he brags especially that he has killed some guy and I don't know what to do." And I said "Well I can't help you with that, I wouldn't tell on my sister." and you can turn him in and tell the cops about your brother and you're going to have to figure it out yourself, anyhow I never seen him anymore, and I'm wondering today what happened to him.

After that I had a son, a little young boy and his father they trained together. That was the youngest black belt that I've ever promoted. I could not promote his father without promoting him, because he was much better in everything than his father was. And I had a little Mexican kid. I'll never forget him. He had him and his sister. I think they lived in Lynwood CA, in this city right next to Compton Blvd. and it was the City of Paramount. He belonged to the gang and I caught him once doing graffiti in Compton and as I said before I'll say it again" Blacks, Samoans, and Mexicans really messed up Compton.

They had graffiti everywhere and walls were broke down, and he smiled at me in the car and when he came back to class I told him that he shouldn't be doing nothing and that he could get locked up you know, and he would ruin his whole life, and his mother she was real sweet real nice, and I said " you have your sister and your mother that you should show your love too, I said "so don't do that no more,"and he never would say nothing smart to me. But one day he wouldn't do his techniques right or nothing and so I told him to go home and get himself straightened out before he came back.

Well I was sitting in my office one day and I think he was mad because his sister wouldn't go with him, he told her come on and she wouldn't go, and she said "no I'm staying I like Master Peterson's teaching," and the mother agreed she called me on the phone and told me "if she wants to stay she can stay." But I went to class the next day and a bullet hole was right down in there,(pointing to the area) well the bullet landed in the wall and that's why it didn't come all the way here, (pointing to the sight) but I saw outside the building a hole in the building, and it was a bullet hole and if I would have, if I would have been sitting at my desk that bullet would have been right between my eyes. So the neighbor next door and I went over and talked with him and they said "yeah we heard shots in fact a couple of shots." So I called the police and they came and they didn't find the bullet but did recognize the bullet hole and we never did figure out who it was. But anyhow just so you know I had a wonderful school there and Tom Hardie and all of them helped me teach.

Every time that I would hold class the newcomers would turn them over to the older students who were there, and that's the way I did it you see and then I would teach the older students something new and so anything didn't get old. And then if I said a youngster or any of them just couldn't do right or won't obey they gotta give me ten more push-ups and they end up bull skating and I see them. They would say "I did my ten Master Peterson " and I would say "okay" and I know they only did five (chuckle) or they laid on their stomach every time (chuckle). But I mean you know even the push-ups would help them give them strength and power. I was so I was very proud of all my students.

Then I left out of that building and the cheese guy was going to do something with that room and I moved to a VFW post and that's where I had to give demonstrations and all that and Tom Hardie would have to do his flying side thrust which he like to do anyhow and spinning wheel kick and I keep hollering and he jump higher and higher and he would do it powerful. I bartended there at the VFW post and what not and I was also the chaplain for many years at the Veterans Foreign Wars building in Compton and I loved that you know.

After I left Compton's best dojo I moved into one down on Compton Blvd. up on the other hill, Compton Blvd. near Wilmington Ave., and that building was real nice and set for the holy roller church (chuckle) and you would hear the drums beating and caring on (chuckle) but I had a lot of fun and the preacher would come over a lot and talk to me you know and we had a ball. But you know it's certain things you gotta put up with, but in that building there ah there's a lot of empty rooms and I wanted to start the organization for the youth in Compton where they could get the best of education. I had retired from electronics from the City of Los Angeles and I wanted to to teach them electronics and I wanted to hire senior citizens that had other jobs probably pay them $500 a month or something like that and they could collect $5 or $10 dollars per student and I had it all planned out, and I made out the format and I made out the flyers and whatnot and my oldest daughter and her husband came to my house they had made up flyers for me and we sorted them out and put out all of those flyers to movie studios and everything you could name all the movie stars you could name and everybody. We tried and I even had the Black Congressional Caucus you know the Black Caucus and I tried everybody that I could get to try to send me some funds and that was in 1984. The Olympics would be going on and I worked with the 1984 Olympics everyday at the same time I was working for the City of Los Angeles Communications Division.

Chapter Eight

Life in the Beautiful City of Compton

I moved to Compton in the year of 1965 when I retired from the U.S. Navy and later purchased a home 1 block from Long Beach Blvd. I stayed there until my beloved wife Esing passed away in the year of 1999. While there she and I would ride to work together since we both worked downtown. She worked as a seamstress in LA's Garment district on 8th Street and I worked at first as an Assistant Electrical Tester for the Water and Power Department where I ended up going house to house testing Electric Meters from San Pedro through Los Angeles.

The great day came along that I was able to take the test for Communications Electrician for all of the departments of the City of Los Angeles. At the time there were only two Blacks in this department and the shop was located near Chinatown, not too far from the Glass House main Police Station then we moved to Crocker Street and San Pedro Street, which was in the heart of skid row. Our workplace buildings were large and I started out working as an installer and repairman of all of the radio and sirens on all Police and Fire Department vehicles.

Soon they gave me the job of working out in the field with the call sign of Service One. During the Watts riots, I suffered a lot of prejudice-ness from the police mostly when the chief of police had hired from the Southerners since he figured they knew how to handle Blacks better than the Northerners. One officer on guard at Wilshire Police Station wanted to stop me from getting the keys to the vehicles I had to work on there even though I showed him my badge and when I walked back out he saw me drive away in my big yellow city tagged truck full of electronic equipment. My boss called the chief and told him that he would not tolerate this type of treatment to any of his workers and these police detectives and whatever had to bring their vehicles downtown to the shop until they got the message.

There were similar run-ins with certain members of the fire department but overall I really enjoyed doing my job either at their many fire stations from San Pedro to the Valley and sometimes upon the mountains where equipment was located. I was a driving repairman fool during the day and the night man would take over for me at night. Soon I was assigned to the graveyard shift and being all alone at night. A night that I will never forget was in 1968. I recall the night all hell broke loose because Senator Bobby Kennedy had been killed in Los Angeles. Sen. Kennedy was the brother of John F. Kennedy and he was running for president of the United States after his brother was killed. I was the only radio technician on duty that night. None of the emergency radio equipment worked at the Rampart Police Station because they did not have an antennae for the emergency transmitter. I was swamped with vehicles awaiting service, until we found out that the main emergency transmitter antenna was the problem. My boss called me and told me help was on the way and for me to remain in the shop and just do what I could. That is what I did, the best that I could. It was a relief for me when help showed up.

In Compton, many white people owned beautiful housing complexes there and Blacks or Samoans were not allowed to even walk through the walled off areas. They did have a black mayor. It was not but a few years after that, when the Salvation Army building was built and I had started teaching Tai-Chi Jitsu Self Defense there in that building in the year of 1967. We observed that many Blacks were moving in and soon as they moved into an area the Whites would move out.

I had a pretty good job repairing and experimenting with the first big computers. Since I was just in training I mostly watched until I caught on to how to follow through all those manuals to trace out a problem. Shortly after starting this job I was on my way home at night and observed many young Blacks running in and out of gas stations filling these bottles with gas. I had a bar I stopped at many nights to get me a shot or two before I went home and all hell broke loose.

The news on the tv said that Watts citizens were rioting, burning up stores, robbing, throwing cocktail bombs everywhere, even at passing cars. A few of these rioters ran in the bar and asked us to come out to their cars or trucks, which was loaded with booze for a dollar a bottle. My car was loaded and every time I went to the barber shop I downed a half pint for a quarter. I had nothing to do with the riots and for some reason it seemed that the rioters respected my area of Compton where I had bought a house, although we did have a couple of guards up on top of our store roof with arms and I had my pistol that got me in trouble later in my glove compartment. It cost me a $400 fine, $500 for a lawyer and almost lost my job if the judge didn't give me a plea bargain warning. I have not owned a gun since and do not want one.

All at the same time I was leaving home making short or long trips (across country) from New York to San Francisco to officiate both at open and/or traditional tournaments which included either the top black belts, their families and their students too many to name. One that comes to mind was at the Cow Palace in Oakland, CA where I was the center Judge for George Chung competing against Stuart Quan for the Grand Championship Trophy.

They performed three different forms each because we could not break the tie. I then asked the promoter to present two trophies which he did. All at the same time I was officiating at all of these amateur boxing shows all over Southern CA. I would go to New Jersey, Georgia, Ohio, New York or anywhere that I was invited to participate in helping out but could not get but very few black belts to come to Compton where I took great losses at giving tournaments.The black belts would come out and tell me that if I gave the tournaments anywhere else other than Compton they would come. So I did give a tournament in Carson, where I thought I had to pay for the gym and my son-in-law who drove the school bus told me he would bring a bus load of youngsters to my tournament. I gave this one to honor the only female master and her husband who hand inducted me twice in their El Paso, Texas hall of fame and once for my Filipino wife Esing.

I gave a demo there of my style and obtained great respect afterwards from this cocky Filipino fighter, master, when after I had decked my own black belt and the stick flew across the floor he charged at me braggartly and ended up on the deck himself with the sticks gone. Later in life when I moved to the Beaumont CA. I was able to assist him many times to run his dojo and officiate at his tournaments with great honors.

The walls of the city started having big holes in them. The yards started being loaded with trash, we could go through instead of drive around. Samoans were barbecuing often. Compton went to hell in a hat basket. Since I was a retired Navy Chief Radioman, WWII and Korea Vet, Self Defense instructor, Grand Knight of the Knights of Columbus and Lecturer at Our Lady of Victory Catholic Church, the principal tried to help me raise finances to start a big youth center and the two people whom I was raised up with in Milford, Ohio were in-charge of the voting procedures. I was asked by them to run for the city council but nothing less than the Mayor of Compton.

My name was so much on the ballot that after my wife begged me not to run. I went to their house and they begged me to please run, since they had no one else really and it looks like I would be a sure win. They found another person at the other catholic church in Compton and he was not only unknown but was elected and died in his second term. In 1976 I started officiating at that time for the AAU in Amateur Boxing shows and was so happy when they later changed the name to USA Boxing and sent a top official to teach us how to judge since we were making a big mess all over the counts. The 10-10 method came in with 10-9 for the winner of a round and 10-8 for one fall. And the referee had to determine whether it was intentional or not.

I did referee practically all of our great Southern CA. professionals today in boxing when they were kids. I traveled to New York (Lake Placid), Denver,CO., or Kansas City, at least 5 times to officiate at five Olympic Trials in boxing. It was at one that I disqualified Macho Camacho Jr. I did not know or care who he was, just three warnings for breaking the rules. His beautiful mother hugged me afterwards. He also did several times after he turned pro. I must tell you how he was about fifteen minutes late coming to the ring. The sun was burning my head up as the timekeeper. The ref was about to disqualify him when he came riding out to the ring on the back of a camel. It took him only two rounds to knock his opponent out, jumped upon 3 sides of the ring, came to my side and froze. He hollered at me, "you were the one who disqualified me from the Olympics" I said " yes and I'll do it again." He hugged me while my wife and I ate together at a casino in Palm Springs, CA.

This type of foolishness reminds me of another boxer who would not follow the rules since he asked me outside the restroom once what were the rules, his coaches had never taught him. I had just rolled him like a barrel across the ring after he would not stop attacking this other good boxer, getting a good beating each time and my hollering at him to stop, break and step back.

After this fight the female official had told me that they had, had a problem with this guy before and saved him for me. The last time I saw him after I disqualified him, after he asked me the rules was when I went to Los Angeles in Inglewood to keep time for pro fights and he was on the card. He knocked his man out in the second round, jumped upon the ring rope to do a backward flip and landed flat out on his stomach. His trainer came straight over to me and told me he was through with this fool, never no more.

Chapter Nine

Established and Teaching in Compton

Okay let me go back a little bit and to every dojo that I had in Compton I would always welcome any black belt in Compton. Master Mat Moore would come and Professor Hugh Macdonald and just you name it any of them they would come, well some would come and try to take over you know because they thought they were high and mighty in the United States and you had to belong to their organization to even have a dojo in the United States. Ah they had a lot of problems with me because I had a couple of letters that I wrote them and they found out they couldn't run me. And now I just tell them I say "this is my style I founded this," and then I would officiate at all from New York to San Francisco.

Every black belt that you could name at that time came under me in judging and officiating and not only did officiating start in Las Vegas, Nevada as they at the Aladdin Hotel the old Aladdin Hotel was the first they ever had us volunteer to fight each other the masters and that was anyone over fifty years old. Oh I walked with that and so on that stage I defeated about 9 out of 12 and on the stage. And I held a trophy and if anyone wants to doubt anything you got to say come to my house in Gilbert, AZ and then we will see if it's the real thing.

Now getting back to my dojos in Compton after I had promoted about 6 or 8 black belts at one of the lower parks of Compton. I had one student that found out where my sifu (teacher) had taken his training. Well there was a Chinese couple in Chinatown that I had never seen myself, so I didn't know who it was and this was the person who taught

85

me Gung fu that I spoke of and that my student went and trained with them. And then he was at a tournament once and I tried to say something to him about what he was doing and he told me "don't you say nothing else to me I'm not under you no more, I'm don't wanna be bothered with you." and I said "well you don't get smart with me like that either," you know and he said "yeah well what you going to do about it?" and he took a swing at me.

The next thing you know he was up underneath the food truck and Kid Jason and the BKF (Black Karate Federation) guys were there. They all pulled both of us out, just drug us out and I took his head and was about to crash the back of his head into the concrete and they jerked me up off of him. He came the next day that Monday to see me. I am very proud of him, he was very good and I'm not gonna even call his name because I don't want to embarrass him, but then he brought all of his belts and put them on my desk very respectful and I said "okay bye sayonara"(chuckle). But he came back later and I said "well are you coming back to training?" and he said "yes". And he went on and made his black belt under me and I haven't seen him in a long time. So he had a girlfriend that also was my student and I just want to mention this because she was killed by gang members and they dumped her body into the Los Angeles River and no water was in it. They took her in the tomb from what I understand and they beat her with something. At her funeral her face was really bad and I never could find out who it was. I inquired at the school and everything else.

As a matter of fact I tried to teach at a few of those schools in Compton well I did teach at one of them, two really. But at the main high school they were like a prison, when you walked outside you heard more profanity and all types of bad conduct and they hollered at me, Are you

Bruce Lee? and all this kind you know making fun of me. When I did have a class there that night it was only about a handful only about five kids came and the rest of them were out there on the playground and you look out there and it was dust dark. It gets dust dark you know for four months of class and as soon as it was over you walk out and they be out there having sex you know (chuckle), and wouldn't think nothing of it. This one guy he rode by on a bicycle and he was heckling me hollering "Kia Kia Kia" and I ran to get the bicycle and I guess I was fast enough and he never (chuckle) would bother me no more, and I guess he said if this man can run after me on this bicycle you know then I'm not that tough (chuckle).

I taught at another school and the principal seemed to be very interested in me teaching there, but I couldn't keep the students. They asked me would I go around to the different classrooms and talk to the classrooms and get them interested. This one classroom especially, they had that I recall all the bad kids in there. the ones that were hard to teach and all that. I walked in the room and this girl was sitting on the lap of a boy and the teacher was up at the desk and she was trying to tell them to keep quiet and they were loud as hell. So I clapped my hands two times like the same way I would do in my dojo. When I clapped my hands two times that means for my students to fall in and lock it. They started clapping their hands two times. I said now, "Monkey do as monkey see. Now why do you clap your hands two times or why did I clap my hands two times?"

They said, "I don't know."

"Well then, why are *you* doing it? You all have better sense than that," and then I asked the girl, "Get out of his lap." She did. She got up and sat over in another seat. (chuckle) I was in my Gi (uniform). I guess I was looking kind of tough I don't know, but they started kind of listening. Now I said, "I am here to start a self defense class and I'm from World War II and the Korean War. Now anyone in here that's interested I would like to have you and I really want to have you better than the ones, the students that are doing good in school because you are tough you understand and I wanna make you tougher okay. I wanna teach you not only how to defend yourself but how to respect yourself and respect others that's it. So if you're interested come and see me tonight."

They said, "Okay" and not one of them I don't think ever showed up, and so I just quit there. There isn't any need in going over there you know.

One thing I wanted to mention was that I was sitting in my office one day and I was in there and my students had started exercising and getting ready for class, and this young fellow came in and he didn't know that I recognized him because I had been shown who he was. But he was the one that was riding on a bicycle once and up on Compton boulevard and snatched my wife's pocket book as he went by on the bicycle and he didn't know when he walked in my office that I knew him and I been looking for him(chuckle) and so I played very coy and ah asked him what he wanted. And he said " I want you to teach me this ah stuff you're teaching here," like that and I said "well ah I don't think you want to learn martial arts and self defense, and I said "I think you want to try to hurt somebody and I don't teach any students that want to hurt somebody." you know. And he said "why do you say that?" And I said "because I'll tell you something young man if you don't get the hell out of my office and leave very quick, I'm going to break your dad blane neck I said " you're the one that snatched my wife's pocket book and she never got it back and I've been looking for you," and he jumped up and quick (chuckle).

Another thing happened this was very funny but then it wasn't funny, there was a lady across the street there that had this big Kentucky Fried Chicken restaurant and she came through the parking lot and I'm standing back here and I was the only one in the dojo and I'm looking. I could look straight out my front door, the front door was open. And I saw this woman just turn around and pull up her dress and put it on the ground and pee like a horse. (chuckle) I went in my office (chuckle) not knowing that she would have nerve enough to come into my dojo, (chuckle) and the next thing I know I heard somebody say "Is anybody here?"(chuckle) and I went out and I said "get out of here quick."(chuckle) And she said "okay". But that was Compton and as I told you that Compton was one of the most beautiful places that you ever want to be.

When I first moved here they've got Harvard you know and so all this time I was living up on South Poinsettia Street which is a better part of Compton next to Long Beach Boulevard and my neighbors and everybody was very nice, and I had one of the brown belts practice with me under a police sergeant from down in the San Pedro area. And he was the sergeant, he knew that I had been into the martial arts for 30 years and he would try to train the others to beat me but he offered his Gold Olympic Medal and to whoever beat the most students that day and it so happened to be me.(chuckle) And I didn't fight the brown belt that I was telling you about earlier.

On my street I personally did not allow any gang members to come down the street and they stayed off the street. I told them one time a couple of them and I started to talk to them and they said who do you think you are? And I said "well if you want to find out then you come through that gate I said otherwise you said why are you picking on me?" I said "because you have all of the mouth." "And you look like you're the one that's the leader of the bunch here."

He said "ain't no bunch here," and I said "I know where you live and there are a bunch of you over there, and I know the old man that you live with, and so I'm going to let you know that if you start anything on the street, and if you don't come over here in a peaceful manner and you mess with these Mexicans like you came and shot up my neighbors van and his house one night." I said "I'm coming over there and I tried to talk my neighbor into calling the police on you. I said "well I'm coming over there personally and y'all will regret it, okay?" And one of the guys said "okay okay okay old man," and so they left but they never bothered to come down again. All of my classes I ended up teaching in my garage because I got put out of the school there and I couldn't get any money to do anything.

I worked the whole L.A. Olympics everyday and like I said everyday in the boxing venue because I was an amateur boxing official and I probably mentioned it before. But in my garage I had a Sergeant of the LAPD and another peace officer that were training with me. Then Tom Hardie and Rickey Greene came to me. I had started teaching Rickey and his football team(I was a strength and conditioning coach) . The football team that his daddy was in charge of and his dad I were VFW veterans together. He was a very wonderful man and " Rickey was a very good football player. He played quarterback I think it was but I was told to come in. I was asked to come and teach the exercises to the guys on the football team. And Rickey hated that and he said "that man is hateful," he said he made you do these exercises and I said "just do them and stop complaining, and he didn't like that and he had an attitude about them and he was the quarterback you know. (chuckle) He finally ah he got into a car accident or something I don't know what, and I never did exactly know what happened to him. But he couldn't pick up his leg and his hip was ruined and what not and he just had it replaced. Ah and he couldn't pick up his foot very little off the ground and his dad brought him to me, and asked me would I teach him and I said "yes I'll teach him the best I can.

He can't do the ukemis (falls) ah he can't fall but I will teach him punching and he said "well that will be good," and kicks, and I will teach him some of the throws and he said "well that will help him out." Well while his daddy's in there talking to me in the office Rickey's standing out there you know his daddy was out of the office and I heard oh no daddy I don't want that man, nah I don't want that man, no parts of him and he said who you talking about Mr. Peterson, I know his voice. His dad said you're going to stay under him, you are going to train soon. Rickey started out with me with his little attitude. The next thing you know he started learning and building Rickey Green and Rickey became a master under me. He was doing fine. He had 4 hip replacements and he used to teach martial arts for the City of Los Angeles. He fell one time and he broke his hip again. He adapted my style in the later years to what he could physically do. He was still training in the martial arts until he got an infection and God called him home.

One evening I was teaching and was so happy to see the greatest brown belt point contact fighter come into my driveway. He cannot talk because he is a deaf mute. He tried, you know but then I found out by his actions and writing back and forth to each other he told me that he wanted to learn my style. I was so happy, we would spar and he would spar with the other students in my garage. He would beat me of course because he was the best. He was really good. He was always pulling on his pants during the sparring. So I said "I have to put a stop to this" so I put my pads on and he was looking at me. I said in a muted voice). "Yeh"so I got one of the other black belts to officiate. I got

3 points on Henry Wilson before he could look around and he shook it off. Next evening, I put the gloves on with him. He takes his gloves and throws them on the ground and starts walking down the driveway. I ran and touched him on the back and said "come here, come here." Took him inside and sat him down. I said Henry you need to stop pulling your pants down, leave them alone and acting all cute when you are fighting. I don't know what happened but he did stop and next time I know he was pointing (scored points) on me. I am happy about this. He learned well and I promoted him to black belt.

Soon as he makes his black belt he goes to a tournament and William Williams is so proud that he beat my fighter, Henry Wilson. The next tournament which was in Culver City a man that I don't think too much of, the center official and I figured William's was going to get cheated. This was the second time I ever stood there and watched my fighter, I was always officiating somewhere while they were competing. But I was always right there at ringside and he was fighting William Williams again and he fought the matches until he fought for first place. He got one point on Willie William's and then Williams went into his dance with his long gi (uniform) coat on (chuckles). He looked over there at me (chuckles) then went on back to fighting when the bell rang. And then Willie William's got another point, now the third point coming up he got it again. One of the judges called and the other one said he didn't see anything. Ron Chappelle was the one I was talking about earlier, and he turns and looks at me, and I said he ain't going to get this point (chuckle) winner Ha Ha Ha. Henry Wilson threw his gloves off and ran and wrapped around me like a baby. Just prior to that fight that he had, that was about the first time also I ever went back there where they were training for the fights and sparred with any of my students. That I did. I went back there and sparred with Henry Wilson and got him more so ready (chuckle). He stayed with me and he made black belt under me, and then he started, and I believe he works for the state now and he's a handicap deputy passing out ah what do you call them cards? You know that you use it for talking to non-deaf people.

Let me go back after that Willie Elam started a school down on Anaheim street in Long Beach, so I went down there and every time I went down there he wanted me to teach. Henry Wilson was taking boxing. He was trying to become a professional boxer and right across the street from Elam's school was the boxing gym where Henry was. I went over there a couple of times and I saw them spar and he was looking good, and he goes to San Francisco and gets knocked clear out of the damn ring (chuckle). We had a big laugh about it and he came to my house but he never boxed anymore though. But what tickled me about Willie, Willie was the sneaker, and he had a good school also in Compton at one time (chuckle). Henry had some good women and I had some pictures of them in the garage and he was doing real great. I have a picture of him kicking a guy 7 " feet tall with a flying side-thrust. Him and my grandson Freddie Perry loved to do it along with Tom Hardie (chuckle). Willie would always try to trick me while Big John would tell me what he was going to do. But Willie had a sneaky way about him at that time.

You know he was the second leader of the Crips and so he had that gang mentality and it's still in him. I knew that, but I'll never forget I was teaching the somersault roll when somebody would throw a knife or a stone at you. You go into the somersault roll and come up right on them and you get control of them. I went to throw the knife (real) at him, he didn't go into the roll he just ducked and picked up the darn knife, threw the knife back at me and I went into the roll on him (chuckle), and surprised the heck out of him. He meant to hit me with that darn knife because he was showing off. He had a couple of other tricks and he would do things like that. I remember that he was in my dojo that I had down on Compton Blvd.

I had another black belt that would come there every so often and run his class because I had to make extra money to keep that building. But Willie would come and he wouldn't pay me extra to teach his students. But he would do the grappling techniques with them on the mat, and I'd be out there just sitting in my office watching them do the grappling techniques, every now and then I'd tell them that that won't work(chuckle) but he didn't like that. Him and Robert wanted to venture off into other activities in the martial arts, so they wanted to learn weapons and all that. I don't teach Samurai swords anything that you can't carry in the streets. I teach the staff I teach the tonfa, I teach the kubaton I teach the escrima sticks only in the defensive techniques.

This type of foolishness reminds me of another boxer who would not follow the rules since he asked me outside the restroom once what were the rules. His coaches had never taught him and I had just rode him like a barrel across the ring after he wouldn't stop attacking this other good boxer. Getting a good beating every time and my hollering at him to stop, break and step back he wouldn't do it. After this fight the female official we had told them that they had a problem with the same guy before and they saved him for me to officiate. This was the first time I had seen him after I disqualified him last and after he asked me the rules was when I went to Los Angeles and Inglewood to keep time for professional fights. And he was on the card. He knocked this man out in the second round and jumped up on the ring to do a backflip and landed flat on his stomach. His trainer came straight over to me and told me I was through with this fool and never no more.

Chapter Ten

The Mountain and then to the Valley

Okay after my wife Esing had passed away in the year 1999 and I had moved to Big Bear, California on a very cold and snowy night my Mexican neighbors helped me all the Black neighbors all they wanted to do was ask me if I had anything to give away in the line of furniture or something. But the Mexican neighbors came and loaded my truck that I rented and drove all the way up there in the middle of the night because we didn't get started until around 12 midnight. And they had to still go to work the next day and lift that heavy furniture. I had one TV that was so big and bulky (chuckle). And I couldn't see how one man could lift it but that one guy he was something else he was very strong. So they got me moved in and once I settled in Big Bear just next to where the kids used to ride the big old inner tubes down the hill in the winter time. And I didn't know it was just a hill. I thought it was a real mountain or something but it was just down from my house.

I had a dog and his name was Mr. Bus and he was very comforting to me. It was just him and I that lived up there. I taught at the same building that the pro boxers trained at. The professional boxers would come up there and train because it was hard to breathe and that air would help them out a lot for when they go back down. I do know that Oscar DeLaHoya had a street named after him there and also had his house and that's where he had his boxing school. Ah he tried to open up a big place for the kids up there, the youth, and he wanted to put in a million dollars, and the East Los Angeles kids and whatnot and the young people there were very mad at him because he hadn't done anything for East

Los Angeles. But the Mayor up there was very funny. He wouldn't let anything go on up there in Big Bear in the line of boxing tournaments, boxing shows, and karate tournaments or anything like that, and I couldn't understand it. He refused Oscar De La Hoya so he went and named his own street and ran his own place. I had a school where I taught Sugar Shane Moseley. They all came up there and they trained there. And Ali's daughter Laila I took a picture of her and she trained there and then my school was right there across the little path and it belonged to the same building as Dr. Les Cohen's place. He rented to me although one day he called me a boy and I said "you're going to call me a boy and here I am renting from you,"(chuckle) so he kind of apologized for his rebel attitude.

It was so cold up there that I had a snowboard trainer and he was from Iceland somewhere over there in the cold climate Greenland or somewhere. Anyhow that was one of the toughest men I've ever seen, strong as a bull and he took my style and he made black belt in my style. But he never did get his citizenship and one time he told me he had to leave the government was kicking him out, and he was married to an American woman but some kind of way they couldn't stay in the United States and I hated to see that.

I had many good students ah well about 9 or 10 to tell you the truth ah that trained with me up there and we put on a show on Christmas. I'll never forget the guy who ran the TV6 they called it up there and he had me do a Christmas show and he told me to show him one of the techniques that I was going to use and so I did the wrist lock on him there (chuckle). And he claimed I broke his wrist (chuckle) and it started paining him a little bit. Oh he complained about that for a long time he was joking with me I don't know maybe he meant it. But you know he was the one that would challenge me and I had to demonstrate that I'm nobody to play with. And when he found that out, the show went over really well. I had about six of my students and I performed. I have a movie of that so one day you might get to see it.

Now, I was also officiating boxing and martial arts tournaments coming all the way down from Big Bear. I was officiating for the State of California and then finally when I got to be older they made me a timekeeper. And I kept time from 2002 until I moved away from Southern California to Arizona. When I was up in Big Bear I used to take my big dog and he was mixed with part wolf and he used to go out into the lake and jump in the lake. I had a long chain and he would go out there after the ducks and then he got out there and sat and looked for me to pull him in, and I said "he can come in by himself" and so I just sat there and waited for him. And then I would take him out into the woods. Oh Mr. Bus was a lot of fun(chuckle), but I think he had a bad heart. I finally had to have his neck operated on because he had a big infection in his neck.

I had a hispanic lady that was renting a room from me once and her son came from Mexico, and I was trying to learn how to speak Spanish and I had this CD and every time I said something they would tell me I'm saying it wrong and all this kind of stuff. The same from when my wife tried to teach me Tagalog (chuckle), and she would always tell me you sound like a Chinese. I asked him to try it out and they told him the same thing so he couldn't even speak English so(chuckle) hardly(chuckle) and so I gave it up. I try often though I have folks now in my wife's family that speak Spanish and also CD's to try to learn Spanish and I can't. I don't know why at the time I wanted to learn Spanish so bad. About five years ago I was a widow and I moved from Big Bear to Victorville and when I moved to Victorville I had a girlfriend. Well, they used to come up to Big Bear but only once or twice because that's the most dangerous drive you want to make and they get sick going up there (chuckle) so they didn't want to come up there no more (chuckle). But I used to have a lot of fun.

One time I went up to Big Bear and I was driving my new, practically new Mercedes Benz and it wasn't even snowing. It wasn't any snow or ice on the road as I knew it. And around this bend the car went by itself I couldn't do anything with it. I tried to stop it by pumping on the brakes until it was safe to stop. I tried to guide it but it went straight over the cliff and I went tumbling straight forward over and then I rolled twice sideways. I had my seatbelt fastened and I was holding on to the steering wheel and I just closed my eyes and said "well God I guess it's my time" and it ended up sitting straight up upside a tree. Well It wasn't too far down because there are big drops up there that's over with. But this one was a little small one it's a park down there, and I sat there for about an hour and a half before anybody came to see me. And the only reason they saw me was because a woman came along and she flipped right in the big where her SUV flipped upside down. I saw her when she rolled and then ah she's turned on her side and started over the cliff and if she had of come over that cliff she would have come right down on me. But she ended up on the road laying on her side, and a guy got out of the car and his wife followed him. I figured it was his wife. Anyhow, he ran and picked her up through a window on the passenger side, and pulled her out of the van. And she was hollering at him to look down, and I'm down there hollering "look down here" (chuckle). He did see me and then he ran down there and helped me out of the car because I couldn't get out of the car. The doors were locked, and I didn't know how to unlock the darn thing and so I'm just sitting there and he eventually figured out how to help me to get out of the car. Thank God it wasn't nothing but the calf of my leg that was hurting. They called the ambulance and the ambulance came, and the nurse came down and she put some lotion or what not on my legs you know and that's all.

The wrecker came, and I didn't know what the wrecker was going to do, but they had me walk all the way up the cliff to the street. And then I went down and sat on the bench, and surprised that I saw them just heist that Mercedes out from down there and put it on a wrecker truck. But then they put me on the wrecker truck and the Highway Patrol came and sent me on my way home. Well when I got home they had dropped me off and told me to report it to my insurance company and what not and do what I could. They told me what wrecker company took it and where they had taken it to. I came to find out it was totaled out. Well, I ended up getting myself a nice Lexus SUV out of that (chuckle) and I was very happy.

My stay up in Big Bear was off and on, because ah I don't know if you know it or not but that is where the Nazis and the White Supremacists and everybody else live up there and if you don't be careful you get in some serious trouble in Big Bear, you know. Because I think they go up there and hide out, and there was one time they didn't allow Blacks up there. I had gone to visit one time, and I went to visit Sugar Shane Moses daddy. He lived up there and on my way up the mountain I was stopped. These guys asked me "where are you going and how long are you going to stay" and all of those kinds of questions. But when I moved up there I didn't have any problem. They didn't see me. I came up the back way.

I moved to Victorville and I would go on trips to officiate and all over the country and I had a girlfriend there for about four or five years. And she wouldn't turn Catholic and so I told her that I wasn't going to marry her and at the same time I had this girlfriend in El Paso, Texas, that I was going to see. And I went there to El Paso to be inducted into this hall of fame and it was run by a female master, the only female master in the Philippines. She and her husband I came to find out that she was after fame and wanted to go into the movies and she felt it was through me that she could get in the movies but she thought I had been in the movies but later found out that I had never been in any movies, and so (chuckle) I kind of surprised her.

I told you before about the tournament that I gave in Compton and it was a flop because I couldn't get black belts to come to Carson or Compton. But then one time I was going to go to a tournament in Georgia, and I was going to drive from Victorville to Georgia. And the lady that I was going with to her son worked at the airport. He was one of the plane loaders or something there. And well he ended up getting in serious trouble by trying to pass dope by a girl going to Chicago and she turned him in, and he ended up in prison.

Anyhow getting back to what I was telling you she told me she said "why do you want to drive when he can get you a cheap ticket on the plane for next to free."

I said "Okay." I forgot that I had my bags and everything loaded.

She said, "All you have to do is drive to the airport and I already called, and he got your ticket already waiting for you." So, I did, and on the route I forgot that I had my gun and it was loaded and I just shot two times (chuckle) but I used to use it for demos. I had a knife in a carry on bag and I had a kubaton and a taser, so the taser wouldn't work but I used it for demonstrations. All of this was in the bottom of this little bag, and I put it up for inspection to go through and the machine immediately showed it. The cops came out and when they took me to the office they were investigating me and everything, and I told them you know I just retired from taking care of your communications, your radio and sirens. Then they checked on that and they found out who I was and as far as that was concerned and they let me go on the trip. And they said "when you come back you are going to have to go to court for a concealed weapon and all that. it took a long time when I got back and finally I went to court and I got plea bargaining and I think I mentioned all of that in what I've written.

Now from Victorville to Cherry Valley, CA I think I stayed there until I moved to Arizona. Before I left Southern California at one of the local casinos they had a big affair for me and surprised me. They called me up to the ring and I got a standing ovation because I had been keeping time for so long and officiating and everything else before I got too old. A lot of my black belts were there and in fact one of the old black belts showed up, Bobbie the one I was telling you about Bobbie Williams showed up and surprised the heck out of me.

Moving to Arizona the weather is hot as heck in fact it is hot right now, and we have sandstorms and all here. And I call myself trying to officiate here but I got one assignment after I got my license and they were very happy to have me and the third day that I was here they had me on the world news and as one of the oldest martial artists in the United States and one of the highest rank. My neighbor was one of the ones who told me about it on the way to the mailbox one day, the third day I was here.

Well that's all I have for my life and also I didn't tell you about how I met my wife Elida. She is Hispanic and a beautiful lady. She has a wonderful family there were eight girls and two boys. And I kept going to see her in El Paso, and I was inducted for the second time in the Hall of Fame and that was where the Filipino Masters who were running the hall of fame she went and got her and brought her there to meet me.

I didn't have much time to even talk to her and what not because they had me sitting up front in the chairs of the guest of honor. But when they started dancing I was able to dance with her and she came to California when I gave a tournament for the same Filipino lady Master and her husband. I took Elida to the Fairplex Fairgrounds in Pomona, CA where they were having the Los Angeles County Fair, I think they call it. Anyhow we were looking at all the animals and whatnot and the different cows and goats and chickens and turkeys and you name it. I brought her a beautiful barbecue dinner and we just had a ball and she fell in love with me I guess finally (chuckle) and she spent time with me at home. I kept going back and forth to El Paso to see her and I asked the girl in Victorville would she marry me and she said "yeah" and I said "you have to turn Catholic" and she said she wouldn't do it. And so I said well, and I went and asked Elida if she would marry and she said "I don't want to marry you."

Now the place I asked her was at the fight the boxer Fernando Vargas the oldest one he was fighting in El Paso and he liked me because I had officiated him a couple of times. He was an amateur and his little boy was crazy about me. He came beating on my leg and caring all the time. He gave me free tickets to his fight in El Paso, well he didn't but his promoter did and his promoter liked the heck out of me.

I took Elida and after the fight was over. Vargas almost lost that fight and he said he told me after the fight he rode up in his limousine and he said "I heard you screaming and hollering at me" and I said "I was because I was telling you to move and get out from in front of that guy and you got knocked on your but"(chuckle) and he said "yeah, I heard you and I moved, an he knocked the guy out and I was so happy for him. Elida and I went walking before we got in the car and went home and she told me she said "she loved me and all like that" and I said "will you marry me?" and she said "no I ain't going to marry you" so I said "why do you want to go with me but you don't want to marry me?" I couldn't understand it.

Anyhow, I said "you're going to marry me", and she didn't believe it but I came back and one day I just made up my mind. I went to El Paso and I went to her house and she told me before you come to my house, remember that my sister is a real Christian and I said "Well I'm a Christian too, I'm Catholic. She said "no they are real Christians", and so I said "okay, whatever"(chuckle). She said "be careful we don't use profanity and tell them you drink and all that" because her and I drink and so she said "be careful what you say in front of them", and I said "Okay."

So I went and met her older sister. She was so friendly and nice and all of them were and she finally asked me what I would like to drink, and I said "a cup of tea."(chuckle) I went there a couple of times and while I was there at that time and she would ask me every time and I would say "a cup of tea".

When we got married it was the funniest thing I went there(chuckle) and she asked me what I wanted to drink and one of her sisters that was at my wedding and she brought a pint of wine because she saw the wine that was at my house in Cherry Valley. She saw the wine at my house or maybe she saw me drinking it too. She just brought me a whole bottle of wine, and came to find out her older sister had wine with me,(chuckle) and from then on we always had a glass of wine, and we had a lot of fun. I moved to Cherry Valley and that's where I took my wife, I mean I took her as a girlfriend and then we got married, and we had a little problem to work out and we got that squared away with the police, and so we married.

Today I'm living here in Arizona and as I was telling you I tried to officiate here and I officiated one time and they held a preliminary meeting and the guy in charge who used to be an inspector, gave a signal to the fight commissioner that he disagreed with me. I corrected him when he made the wrong mistake. I guess I wasn't supposed to talk. I was later contacted and told that I was not needed anymore. The judges wanted to be able to override the referee at any time. When I was informed of this I took off the patch when called by phone and refused to further officiate. And I guess I wasn't supposed to talk (chuckle) so I told him I didn't care to officiate anymore if I can't have a say so I won't participate and everything like that.

I also attended a couple of boxing studios here, and one of them is my nephew through my wife, the guy that runs a Taekwondo school. The guy in charge asked me what I wanted to say and if he let me say something and he was very disrespectful. I told him that it was none of his business what I wanted to say. I thanked him for showing me more respect and he said "Well I am asking what are you going to say to my students if I let you talk, and I said "well just forget it". And he did (chuckle) because he kept the thing I noticed was when his students would be fighting with all this protection and all and some of them would be running in and out of the building. The parents were doing all the coaching and what not, and they were saying "kill him, slap him, kick him, you learned better than that, come on" and I told the wife I said "let's get out of here".

Well, then I went pass another dojo that's right up the street from me and it's Karate, and they had a sign out there I think it was $39 dollars for three weeks and your uniform is included, and also they had where you could go to summer camp take the kids to summer camp or something. But I passed there a couple of two or three times, and sometimes I would see little kids coming out and look like they're about 9 or 10 or maybe not even like that old. Because the parents would have their arm around them while they're laughing and going on. And got their Black Belts on and you know, and got sickles or signed samurai swords, and whatever you know right in the streets there walking out. I said "oh my God look at this" (chuckle) and so I gave up.

I went to Walmart and they had a Karate school there and the senior instructor there was very respectful, and I gave him my card and he let me talk to his students, and I introduced myself and he told me that he had been training and was a student of Grandmaster James Mitose. I told him that's fine like if I come here to try to start a dojo I would like to have you assist me. Well when I moved here to Arizona they were gone. That place is pure empty and I haven't bothered with teaching at a martial arts school anymore since I was here other than that.

Chapter Eleven

Through the Eyes of Dr. Danny Layne

A proud Dr. Danny Layne at his training center with some of his students many years ago.

I came way back in the seventies. At the time I was a senior student under Guru Danny Inosanto and I met Soke at the Long Beach International Tournament. I was a brown belt and he worked with me all the way to obtaining my grandmaster status. The thing I want to let you know was originally his Gung Fu instructor was James Sharp. What he taught Soke and me was real. Soke Peterson was a head arbiter but he was also fighting. During the early part of the seventies, and one of the things that Sharp really worked with him on was his blocking, none of the competitors his age wanted to go against him, because his blocks were too darn hard. And I saw him go against almost everybody, and they started to say ouch, ouch, you hurt me. It wasn't so much that his blocks were affecting them, but it was his elbows they were too darn hard. And so later on I asked him, I said, "what in the world" and later on we experienced that at the very first gym in Compton. And he showed me what he was doing, because he was hurting me in practice. So I then realized and decided to study with him.

In 1966 for one month he was trained by Hugh McDonald in Gung fu, where he was requested to spar with most of the students, including a show-off visitor from Bruce Lee's dojo. It was during one of these sessions that he blocked and grabbed a Mexican Football player's ankle when he threw a roundhouse kick at him. Soke Peterson was taking him down when this opponent fell across his leg, popping his right knee cap instead of straight down.

Peterson would continue going to every class, sitting and watching with his knee in cast. He was promoted to Blue Belt, after testing this way. Master James Sharp took over the class and Peterson not only made Black Belt under him but also had established his own style and opened his own dojo (school) at the new Salvation Army building in Compton, CA.

During the time that he was handicapped he wrote the instruction book on Tai-Chi Jitsu Self Defense. He had a lady friend of his edit the book. She was a caretaker and assistant to one of our Black U.S. Congress members. Several of his students at the Salvation Army and VFW Hall in Compton followed him to his great dojo on Compton Boulevard, and White Street. Which was labelled Tai-Chi Jitsu Academy of Self Defense. Many Black Belts visited his dojo there and several trained there in his style.

It was at this time that the martial arts dojo that many Black Belts were not only permitted to compete, teach and but party every day in the city of Compton. Some of the names of well-known martial artists teaching and training were Big John Robertson, James Culpepper, Nat Moore, Hugh McDonald, James Sharp, and Joel Slickster. Many Orientals and Hispanics such as Ted Tabura and Big Al Gonzales spent time there also. Many learned judo, jiu jitsu techniques to add to their expertise and taught my students as their own.

Soke was also responsible for introducing us to the fighting circuit, everybody you could name including the Black Karate Federation (BKF) all of them and they were headed under BKF Steve Sanders, but now he's Steve Muhammad. Okay, needless to say, I wanted you to know that the very first black belter, now I earned my second degree black belt in 1978 under Peterson. I was fighting and everything, and at that time Big John Robertson, and James Culpepper, were fighting. All of us were studying the same style under Master Peterson, at that time, and it was just awesome.

Now, I saw the two major fights that really inspired me, when he fought a guy nicknamed the Fighting Grandpa. The Fighting Grandpa was very famous, he was from the Lancaster area, and an Anglo fighter, he was the same age as Soke, at the same time. He would always be noted as a black belt and a rated fighter and competed internationally all the way through. I saw Soke literally obliterate him, I said, "okay now I know he knows what he's doing". And we studied and all of us would fight together, Big John and Culpepper and myself became close. Culpepper was a champion from the east coast originally, and so that's how we had heard about Soke, so we all said, "we're going to be fighting the BKF, and all those from Los Angeles.

At that time, it was an Hawaiian fellow that was real sharp, and was the number one fighter all the way around from the Islands. He was under Steve Fisher. His fighters would only show up at his school and fight just to be fighting. They didn't really care about the kata's or any of that, they just wanted to score as top fighters. He had top fighters and so was Steve Fisher around that time as an instructor.

Peterson was knowledgeable about head judging and arbitering, and there was another top fighter by the name of Winter's, I forgot his first name. There was a fighter, that was all in the valley, who took everything, and so he was bragging about how bad he was, and nobody would fight him. So, at this one big tournament, Soke said, "I'll fight you", and at the same time, I was right there, and I'm thinking, "oh sure he's going to really fight him". He was putting on his mitt and gloves and all that, and the shoe gear, he was padding up, and I said, "okay now this is going to be interesting". This guy is the champ of the champs and he claims to and he's won this international tourney and I want to see what my instructor does. Sure enough, I saw him fight Winter's and it was close in the first round, real, real close. Then all of a sudden, the second round came, and I saw Peterson, come right through and knocked him with the back knuckle punch, and in Chinese, instructors call it Kwa Chui. Ah, the same thing back knuckle punch, and I was wondering what he was doing that really hurt him. Well, he knocked Winter almost out, and he did the back knuckle punch, done with his knuckles sticking out. So the minute it made contact, it slipped through his gloves and "bam"! He hit him on the side, it was incredible, and needless to say, I said, "okay so that's what the back knuckle punch is all about".

During those days, you know Muhammad Ali used to do the same thing. He used to angle out swift, and then circle, and then while he's back peddling he would be hitting you with the back knuckle punch. We used to call it, like I said the "Kwa Chuis", and with some time and patience with inside out and it worked. And, I saw with a lot of the competitors that I had done, now one thing that Steve Sanders used to teach, and this motivated Culpepper to really study under them and fight. We used to get together, while we were preparing, and Soke would get us in shape over the weekend and everything. He would get together with a lot of BKFers (Black Karate Federation practitioners). Under Sanders this was before he became Muhammad, he would work with timing. So that is when my eyes open up and I said okay. It is more than just combinational power, it's about timing. What Sanders used to do is teach Culpepper how to slide in and move the timing, but hide his, the approach of moving inside of your opponent. I got under that real quick. He loved working with me and that brought up my level as well.

Soke not only catered to Sanders and let me tell you about what Soke did. He never would say well you know like what some teachers would say only stay at our school, he didn't do that. You guys are going to be fighting the BKFers so I not going to hold back. I am encouraging you to go and see what they do. The situation was that among the fighters there was camaraderie with a lot of the fighters. The Hollywood experience thing attracted a lot of the good fighters there.

Many of the BKFers, the real BKFers that were under Sanders, were actually in the movie "Enter the Dragon" with Jim Kelly. When you look at that scene again and when you look at Steve Sanders giving Jim Kelly a signal, watching a lot of those guys were in it. They were real students under Sanders. Guess what ? All of those guys we had an opportunity to meet, talk with and at some point, fight. If you ask me if Soke was selfish in one way in saying "Don't get together with these boys nah! He was just the complete reverse. But one thing that he did want us to note is that his techniques actually were real. His techniques were awesome and if you could pull it off it would not be pulled off inadvertently it would be pulled off because you practiced them in practice.

He believed that in order to really apply the stuff that no matter what the techniques were you had to do it in practice, you had to do it real. And that was also Steve Sanders' application. So he said look you don't even have to throw any major outside things. He said get ready suddenly and work within your technique, within your guard and slip through the guard of your adversary and be there. Throw whatever combinations you want whether inside or angling out. That is what he taught.

The BKFers were more not into the traditional kumite. They were into real combat and real individual fighting. So out of those fights you had your big stars that came out of there during that era like Alvin Prouder who was probably one of the top fighters from his (Sanders) school. He was more than a point fighter, he was a full contact fighter. He fought Jerry Bell and a lot of the old guys. Soke was a world-class fighter. He fought guys from all over. Every so often at the big tournaments he would be rated international grandmaster and we would all have to fight him and that was what motivated me.

I was practicing in Soke's dojo before he got there and I was working with power, timing and thrust power. I was so motivated that I not only kicked a 100 lb. canvas bag that was hung up from the ceiling with springs. I kicked a hole through the bag. Later on I thought Oh my God I'm probably going to be kicked out of the school, get thrown out of the school. I thought I was going to have to pay for the thing. I kicked it off his roof. I thought for sure I was going to be reprimanded and kicked out of his school. But he looked at me and I told him the minute when he walked in the door I told him what happened and he smiled. He was so proud that he started introducing me. He said my student right over there knocked a hole into the canvas bag. And he looked at me and said "What the hell did you kick it with? I laughed and told him that it was your training. He is a real teacher and a real instructor. You can quote me on that.

The other instructor that came from the San Diego side that was very good was another champion. He was probably the best in timing of all time. Even better than Prouder, he probably did not have the power that Alvin did but he had the timing, the essential timing that Steve Sanders had. Sanders had more but there was a guy Orned Gabriel nicknamed "Chicken Gabriel." He was one of the best fighters all the way around. He was awesome and after I moved back here from Hawaii I went to a tournament and there I saw him. I hugged him and was so glad to see him. I knew that Soke was an official, an arbiter of the tournaments and I didn't know at that time that he was a sincere raja-sanctioned instructor and a head arbiter of all the major big tournaments. That was when I learned that he was a lot heavier than I thought.

What I mean by Raja-sanctioned, there was a group of instructors regardless of where the tournament was whether it be western, a sectional, a LA open tournament, a state, international, or a world-class international, Peterson was definitely on top of that. People would ask him literally if he would participate. This was called raja-sanctioning. He was the #1 raja-sanctioned judge, head arbiter of all the major tournaments.

I don't give a darn what star, what full contact champion was there whether it be Alvin Prouder, Howard Jackson, Benny Urquidez, whether it was Eric Lee, I don't care what international fighter or star was there, they all knew Peterson. I saw this with my own eyes. During that time I was still a senior student and still under Danny

Inosanto's School. I did want that personal touch training, coaching on timing, on positioning, on flipping, on grappling, and on Jiu Jitsu definitely from Soke. I was training under Danny Inosanto but I wanted to know the traditional Japanese Jiu Jitsu that Soke learned.

During those days there was another major tournament that was put on by the great famous Mike Stone. Now Mike Stone also studied under Bruce Lee and knew Danny Inosanto. Mike Stone was originally from Lahaina, Maui and that is where I lived for many years. One thing about Mike Stone, he started what was called the Four Seasons competition. And the Four seasons competition featured Soke Peterson as the head arbiter because of his extensive knowledge.

There were all kinds of famous instructors that would come and participate at the Four Seasons and the international bouts. That meant that grandmasters like Sho Kosugi competed. He was known for his sword work, he introduced his son, Shane Kosugi and he raised him up to be a major competitor. I learned Sho Kosugi was born Chinese but he took a Japanese name because the companies that helped make him famous were Japanese. And I learned that from the premier Grandmaster Wayne Yee who was raised in Shanghai, China. He also taught gung fu and gave me special sanction. Peterson knew and studied also under Wayne Yee, but Wayne was fascinated with Soke Peterson's Jiu Jitsu. So as trade off and one thing about it what Wayne told me personally is Sho Kosugi who is famous all over the world for Japanese arts. Sho is taken after a Japanese name but by blood he is really Chinese.

Both Soke and I earned our 5th degree under Wayne Yee too who was born in Shanghai, China. It was Wayne Yee who spotted the genius of Soke's jiu-jitsu. A lot of people underestimated how effective his jiu-jitsu and his wazas were. His kick-boxing, his timing was real and I taught my students that discipline in Hawaii as I was working with a youth group and was given an opportunity to lead them into international competitions. We competed in a tourney run by Grandmaster Junior Ulangaa who threw a big tourney in Oahu that featured an Australian team. My stepdaughter actually became a world champion at the tournament based on using the fighting discipline and techniques I learned from Soke Peterson.

There were two other grandmasters that loved and respected his judgement calls and his ability to make critical calls as a judge and arbiter. Heel Il Cho was a noted Korean traditionalist who loved and respected Soke and was known for fighting and prowess at breaking bricks. To give you an example of Soke Peterson's heart, a famous practitioner that Soke Peterson made an impact on was Soke Takayuki Kubota, who is the inventor of the Kubaton self defense keychain. Kubota left Japan to come to America for the first time and Soke Peterson was the only one to receive him when he came off the boat. No one took the time to make him feel welcome and give him direction but Soke Peterson. Soke welcomed him into his home and fed him. Soke Peterson showed him love and respect.

Some 25 years later at a Kubota tournament in East Los Angeles when Peterson walked in, Soke Kubota stopped the tournament and cried when Soke Peterson walked in. His eyes teared up and he gave Soke Peterson the biggest hug. When I saw that...I knew more than ever that Soke was the real deal. Kubota was sincere and genuine toward Soke. He never forgot what Soke Peterson did for him. I came to see it was about real love, respect and unconditional acceptance for the martial arts. I will never forget the experience.

Other renowned martial artists that Soke Peterson had opportunity to work with included from Hawaii, Grandmaster George Duarte and Grandmaster Ron Perriera tore off their grandmaster patches and gave it to me following my performance in a tournament. Senior Grandmaster Ed Parker, Ted Tabura and Eric Lee who is still known as the King of Kata and even his teacher the great Al Dascascos along with Fumio Demura who was internationally-known were all great martial artists that Soke Peterson got to know. Gracie Casillas, Cynthia Rothrock and Claire "Wonder Woman" Blair and DiAnn Johnson were some of the great competitor-teachers that Soke came to know well. They respected him as an arbiter and a friend.

Soke also spent a number of years refereeing and time-keeping with many in the professional boxing world including the olympian and former world champion, Oscar De La Hoya, along with former world champion Timothy Bradley from Compton. Soke even had an opportunity to teach Venus and Serena Williams as youngsters but their dad, Richard Williams insisted that they stay with tennis and we know how that worked out.

Peterson was a great teacher because of his passion and his understanding of the history and the roots of the Arts. He believed as martial artists that we should know history. Soke Peterson appreciated and recognized the importance of ring savviness and talent but he shared there should be a naturalness expressed in our souls as students and practitioners.

Chapter Twelve

Questions & Answers with Big Cat

During one of many sit-downs with Soke Peterson he was asked a series of random questions. However, his responses were anything but random. Here is a sample of questions and answers that provide a little more insight into the heart and mind of this man.--T.H.

(Q) Dr. Peterson I just have a few questions that I would like to ask you. Why did you first take up boxing?
(Answer): I took up boxing because I had all of my street fights and what not, actually ah as I told you Mr. Henson was one of the men I stayed with; he wanted me to be a boxer under him if he adopted me as a son like he wanted to do. I wanted to learn how to defend myself better because a lot of times I would get my tail whupped (chuckle) and even this girl shoved me down from the back I told you about and I messed up my nose and my face. A lot of things like that because I was an orphan and I felt a lot of the other kids picked on me and so on. So I took it for self protection.

(Q) What led you to learn the Martial Arts?
(Answer): In the Martial Arts that actually came when I went to Moffett Field, California after that horrible boot camp they had(chuckle) remember I told you about before. I fell in love with Judo and Jiu Jitsu that was taught to us by the First Marine Raiders; they were the ones that won the war in the South Pacific. I never gave up on learning all I could from any books I had or anything else I could get my hands on. In fact I bought me a couple of beautiful books and one of them was judo and Jigoro Kano's Ju Jutsu Judo which is actually the name Jiu Jitsu. And also I was given the oldest book at the Cow Palace in San Francisco, I was

telling you about. I just took a great interest in learning all I could and wanted to be taught more.

(Q) *Could you talk about your obstacles that you may have encountered when you first got started in the martial arts, or when you started teaching here in California?*
(Answer): I ran into some prejudice because back in that time even though they tried to stick to regulations. But because you were black they might give you certain assignments. There were times when I was not allowed to be a referee but only a judge even while I was an assistant instructor with John Ogden's Judo in Long Beach, CA. But when they found out that I would not tolerate such a thing as that. I have been known to officiate twenty-one fights in one day. They were amateur bouts and there was no other referee available (chuckle) at the time. God works in mysterious ways, now as I went to officiate and time-keep and all like that well I was able to overcome the prejudice in many different ways. Because when you do a good job I don't care what it is then you want what you know and your work speaks for itself.

(Q) *Now we would like for you to talk about the Watts Riot in the 1960s that pivotal decade of the Civil Rights in this country and that period in your life. Can you talk about how it impacted you as you grew in the martial arts and the experience you had back then?*
(Answer): I never participated in the marches or anything like that ah my Filipino wife wouldn't let me and my daughters either. But I did have a time once during that with my baby daughter she had her "afro" and she was getting into it. Because she was going to Biola Marymount College and her boyfriend that later became her husband he was the founder of the Black organization at Marymount.

She was deeply involved in the affairs and things and all. I finally had to (chuckle) correct her and I talked to her all I could. She was putting things on the wall pictures and crap. And so the prejudice and things we've got to overcome with love and respect for each other. I told her that when you get too deep off the one end, and then that's the same as the Klu Klux Klan. They are just a group of people who are too deep off into one end, the White Supremacy, and we have to live in this world we were all created by God, and we've got to see something good in each other, you know. We don't have to go along with everything that each one of us do because we have our own customs, our own traditions but we've got to get along.

(Q) I think you answered my question, and I would imagine that as a Black man, a martial artist of color you may have had to go above and beyond at times?
(Answer): Many times in fact I had Orientals that looked down on me because here's this guy that is supposed to be one of the top martial artists in the country, and they heard about me and what not but not when I would go to the tournaments they did not recognize me. But now some like Master Yamazhaki would sit up on the stage and just let me run his whole tournament, and he actually told me "take over my tournament Master Peterson and I'll observe." I wanted to officiate but I never did officiate in the ring and whatnot. And it was due to that point and I remember Master Calla Wallace was from Hawaii and I officiated in Hawaii and even though one of my grandmaster's had taught over there I guess he didn't think that a black man should be officiating and he didn't know anything about me, but I would go and work his tournaments for him, and he always said I did a good job. Well one day he just came out and told me he said I have no proof or nothing about you and I probably don't need it but others are asking who

are you and why are you this and that? I said well okay, and so the next time I went he gave another tournament and I was there and he took him a nice write up. He said "I don't want that I don't want to look at it." I said "well it's up to you, and I said you are the one that asked for credentials and I brought them." and from then on he respected me. He came as an old man and we went to a promotion for one of my black belts from Whittier,CA and he was making his master's rank and he was sitting there and I told them I said "one of the things that we do, whereas you all punch each other in the stomach. When you make a master rank we stomp each other."

I laid down on the floor and I called the biggest man in the entire audience to have him come up and stand on my stomach and then I told him to jump on it, and I looked over there at Master Calla Wallace and his eyes were bulged (chuckle) and at that time I was about 85 or 86 years old.

(Q) *Could you share your Brown Belt experience back in 1946 on the tatami?*

(Answer): Yes, back in 1946 we had just got back from duty while stationed at Moffett Field and I'm going to a tournament there in Northern California. I was in San Francisco, the Orientals instructors there were pretty high and mighty (chuckle). They didn't appreciate any other Blacks or Whites to come around the tournaments and what not but I would do it. They did not want anyone from Southern Cal. to officiate at Northern Cal. tournaments. Although my good friend, Grandmaster Hughes, who was in charge of the officials in Northern Cal. was always happy to see me.

I finally wanted to be trained by this Japanese instructor who taught on the base and he never even spoke to me or nothing. I was the Chief Steward and he had no respect or what not but he had me just do exercises and that's all. One day he called me to come and be uke but it was against a black belt (chuckle) and this black belt threw me all over the place. And every time a black belt would come to the dojo I would observe him and wanted to fight with him, and they would throw me all over the place (chuckle). So this one particular time was in San Diego and I remember clearly it was at the Marine base there and this black marine, he was a black belt and he came. And I asked him "let me throw you one time because I want to impress this Japanese instructor there (chuckle), who's been ignoring me all the time and won't even speak to me. And he said "no, you don't touch me," and I reached out for him and oops there I go again and all I had to do was reach for him. He took me to his house and he showed me he had a library just full of books on Jiu-Jitsu and Judo, and he said "come on in here and read and I will help you all you want." He told me you don't touch a black belt he said "I don't know if you know it or not but a black belt is strong but a junior not yet, he gotta give up his belt, and I said oh okay and so I learned a lot by going over there.

One day while I was still a white belt in judo the master had me go up against a brown belt? The master told me to fight him and I said "okay" And I don't know after all of that falling and carrying on, busting my tail, soaking my butt in ice water and what not (chuckle). All the pain one day on that day it came to me what he had already tried to show me by getting the fear out of falling. Once you lose the fear of falling you can fall on concrete, wood, bricks or anything you don't worry about, you just, what they call flying. And once it happened, all of a sudden I put on a Ippon Seoi Nage on him this brown belt and he went flying through the air "bam" and he got up and he said "you ain't going to do that again," and he went back to his corner and

I went back to mine. He ran up and I did it again and he got up and went straight up to the master and took his brown belt off and I never saw anything like it. The master called me and he said "Peterson", and he motioned for me to come to him. I said "yes master", and he said "you did it", and from then on he talked to me and instructed me and what not, but he didn't stay long and that was one of my best experiences.

(Q) *Can you name some of the notable athletes that you trained or officiated over the years?*
*(*Answer): Yamazaki, Tall Bear from Nevada he complained even to his death that they didn't call it right , George Fisher, Dave Parker, Calla Wallace and just about every black belt you could name Stewart Kwong and his sister, all of the BKF fighters, Barry Gordon, Alvin and Cynthia Prouder, the athletes in the Olympics the great black tennis player I often wonder about her because she was a girlfriend in the Walnut Hills area in Cincinnati and we would meet after work to go back and forth to catch the bus to our different venues. Althea Gibson and her last name was the same last name as my mother and they both come from Georgia. And my mother was a Gibson and I don't know about Althea, and she was acting like she couldn't remember too many names. But there was a girl that I went just social (chuckle) with. You know I was at the age of about seventeen or eighteen and she would come over and we would talk while sitting on the porch together. And she was a great tennis player on Ashton Street Park. and we left each other and I asked her once on the way to the bus if she was the one and she said I might have been. I don't know (chuckle). And anyhow Sugar Ray Robinson and Sugar Ray Leonard and he was at the Olympics talking to me once, and the guy in charge said I had a job to do (chuckle).

Sugar Ray told him "hey this is a friend of mine he stayed with me as a child and we can talk as long as we want"(chuckle) and the guy walked away. It wasn't that big of an assignment anyway.

(Q) *Is it true that you have history with former NBA (National Basketball Association) star Cedric Ceballos?* (Answer): Oh yes, he is like a grandson to me he was raised up with my grandsons back then they were just like brothers. He calls me granddad and also his mother. She tried to train with me along with my middle daughter and you know I mentioned that before and I kicked them out. (chuckle) They laugh about that today, the two old women and you know when I say lock it well then I meant lock it. I gave you a chance to lock it. If you didn't you would have been gone. (chuckle) And another one Shaquille O'Neal "Shaq" and the girl who was a martial artist a heavy contact fighter she was a black girl and I can't think of her name right, but she was at a bout and it was something about the bout. I wrote to Washington and told them that they can't mix apples and oranges you know. The athletic commission and I told them that they can't mix apples and oranges and if they keep doing it somebody was going to get killed. And sure enough that next morning one of the fighters while I was not the timekeeper there was someone else. I was just sitting there spectating and me and one of my black belts and I told him I said "that boy is going to get killed because the Russian fighters knew Judo very well and they were strong, big strong guys. And every time the guy would kick or punch at him he would throw him and the guy would bounce on that mat and it was hard you know what I mean. His head would fly back and bust, they had to carry him out of the ring and he never came back. And the next morning it was in the paper that he had died, that same evening I was walking back from the restroom to my seat and this girl was one of the full contact fighters I can't remember her name. But she was talking to Shaq and he had a factory in Compton and I had taken him one of my resumes and asked him to help run this program for the education thing and athletic program for the youth in Compton. I was requesting that he give a donation for it and they put it in the file. I think it was a circular file, I never heard anything, but he did remember my name and it was mentioned to him. And he said "Oh Master Peterson" and that was far as that went. And the news reporters I knew were some of the news reporters.

There was Jim Hill, the sports reporter. He touched me once behind my back. You know he talked to me and I was proud that he did that you know and I knew him well. There was the news reporter in Compton that used to run on the track team at Compton College. And I would go over there and in fact I even raced with one of them guys in football and he ran backwards while I ran frontwards (chuckle) and I couldn't beat him going frontwards to the finish line.(chuckle) Well he had so much fun, this person went to the Coliseum with me once and I wasn't working for the state and I had just paid my way to see the kickboxing show they had there. And sure enough Chuck Norris came up and looked up into the balcony where we were sitting and he said "Master Peterson"(chuckle) and he froze. I couldn't think of anything else to say to him and so I said "when are you going to put me in one of your movies?" And he stood there and said "you know I am going to think about that (chuckle). And he just kept looking, and Chuck never wanted his students to participate unless I was the official at any tournament, and he was also the little blonde haired fellow when we started the full contact. It was Danny Rodarte and I that started that.

(Q) Did you work with the Williams sisters, Venus and Serena?
(Answer): Yes, the Williams sisters used to play tennis when they were kids and practiced tennis down here at the one I call the dope park down there in Compton. And I knew their father Richard very well. He worked for the City of Los Angeles and I talked to them many times and I went to their house. I tried to get him and his wife both to let them come and be in my school that I had down on Compton Blvd. but they were more interested in tennis and they had the little green balls laying everywhere, and the dope pushers there wouldn't let them alone and he finally took them to Florida to train and thank God he did (chuckle).

(Q) Are there any close friends in the martial arts that you had to say goodbye to because they went on to glory?
(Answer): Oh, there was the great one Professor Hugh MacDonald, Brian Breye, Ted Tabura, a great friend of mine, although in the beginning we didn't start off as friends it had to be proven. I used to go to all of his tournaments in Laughlin, NV. and help out. I just did that I would always put myself on people. He used to always have his tournaments during the day and then in the evening he would have his show. You know his fashion show and what not. I went and I sit right up front I'm high ranking I'm thinking that I would be recognized he had the nerve enough to ask me to move so Chuck Norris could sit in that seat. (chuckle) And Chuck was a baby to the martial arts and he and I go back to 1963, and I started teaching in 1947. But he started coming to our affairs, the Black affairs and what not quite often he was always right up under me and I loved him. My good friend, the late Moses Powell, You and I attended his funeral and Moses inducted me into his hall of fame. You know I have been in six halls of fame.

Master Griffith, one of my dear friends, worked for the City of Los Angeles with me and I gave a demonstration at Griffith Park for the City of LA, and I believe you were in that demonstration but I know Bob and I think Rick was in it too. But anyhow it was a big demonstration and they had this one guy who insisted on doing some breaking (breaking boards in half).

And he didn't belong to me but he just volunteered to pop up and do breaking, and what tickled me was (chuckle) one of the kids got up and just touched the board and it just popped.(chuckle) And I made a big mistake to take a purse from the audience and use it in a demo (chuckle), and we were taking videos and what not of the performance that I had my students do. And I called anybody up from the audience who wants to come up and learn something. And this guy I found out was the son of one of my coworkers and after the event he was bragging about how his son beat my butt. Or lock me on the mat and I couldn't move, well what had happened was that I threw him and he used to wrestle. I had a lock on him and he couldn't get out of it and I said okay and I tapped him and I let up. And as soon as I let the wheels over on top of me see here I am under him and trying to get him to move, and I said "hey that's enough" and he continued to try to do this wrestle and lock me down. So I bump my butt up in the air and he comes flying over on top of my head and his head hits on the tatami and if the mat had not been there then his head would have hit right down in that dirt hard because I mean I had enough. And before that while he was doing all this struggling trying to hold me and put a lock on me the crazy audience and women especially hollering "oh he's got him, look at him and he's supposed to be a master ha ha ha." And I had heard enough and I had to handle it(chuckle) and I almost but that dude's head and when that happened the whole place was quiet, because they didn't know if I busted his head or not they saw it hit on the mat. And that was in the video and he went to work bragging to all my fellow employees that his son beat my butt at the demonstration. And so I brought the video to work one day and I called just him and I didn't call anybody else and I showed him that I saved your son and I didn't want to bust his head open.

(Q) I want to ask if I could name some years or decades and you can tell us in a sentence or a few words what was the most memorable for you?

(Answer): Okay in 1979 I started training at Bird Williams Athletic Club the same stable with Ezra Charles as a lefty lightweight boxer and also in that same year or maybe 1940 I was a Cross Country runner first place for the High School and third place for the City of Cincinnati and winner at the City Meet and Cross Country in my second year in High School. In 1943 I enlisted in the United States Navy around April or may because I think in June I was on my way to the South Pacific for World War II had to have been around that because I trained at Moffett Field for a while after boot camp in Norfolk. In 1945 I got married in the Philippines at the end of the war and in 1947-48 I believe I had brought my wife and babies back to the United States. That's after I had started teaching Judo I hadn't found the form of Jiu-Jitsu yet. Also I was sparring and boxing around that time. Oh, I'll never forget I was sparring one day and I was sparring with about three different guys and this big guy came up and he asked me if I would teach him and I was cocky and I told him yes. Let's see what his name is. Oliver Hill or something like that and one day when I went back to the Philippines to get my wife. I flew through Pearl Harbor and he was there and he was going to fight that night, and he told everybody in the

Officer's Galley that this was the man that got me started in boxing. But what he didn't tell them was and I'm glad he didn't and that was that he hit me so hard my head hit the wall, (chuckle) and you know he was a middleweight and I was a lightweight and I was still so he woke me up. I was supposed to have been teaching him and bop. (chuckle) And I told him I said "You're going to make a great boxing champ and sure enough that night when I went to see him fighting in Pearl Harbor I didn't have nothing to do with the fight except he had told everybody that I was his instructor.

I was leaving out the next morning heading to the Philippines and he beat that guy that he was fighting so bad they had to jump up in the ring and take him off of him. The referee was trying to stop him and the guy was out and he was still beating him down. His own secondary coach had to jump and get him. He was something else I think he went on to win the middleweight championship in the South Pacific and that was 1947. In 1950 I was in Portsmouth, VA, and that's when my baby girl was born at the Navy Hospital in Portsmouth, VA and we had just come back from a tour of duty in Jacksonville, FL where I was shore patrol there for these two years and didn't even have to report to base. Black Shore Patrol Officers could only patrol black areas in Jacksonville. They had to have their office in a room over the top of a pharmacy store there. I was a lefty pitcher on an amateur team and three of the Jacksonville Eagle ball players came and they were just playing around with us and they didn't even know that I was in the Navy. And they couldn't hit. They couldn't get the ball out of the infield, and when I had played the game that Sunday I had thrown my arm out. And I couldn't do no good and they were on the back side looking at me to decide if they wanted me on their team and I couldn't get the ball over the plate because my arm was so sore from that practice game. (chuckle) My wife and kids stayed in Portsmouth, VA. and my kids were raised up there and I was on many ships and in fact I was on ten different ships, and four half stations and I ended up in Boston, Rhode Island and then that 's when I changed my route and came back to Norfolk. I changed my duty station and my best buddy. He thought I was trying to show off and I went on to school with him. I got orders to go to San Diego and it's all in there.

(Q) What about the fifties?
(Answer): I bought my first TV in 1950. My wife and I had credit all up and down High Street in Portsmouth,VA. and we didn't have much money. I put it on the credit card and she worked. She did seamstress work and she would build tents for the Army and she worked. Because of the credit we had didn't want for anything. I purchased a large TV to watch Joe Louis fight.

(Q) During the sixties did you start teaching in Compton?
(Answer): I started teaching in Compton in 1967 I moved there in 1965 it was in 1966 when I started taking Gung fu during the time that my knee was in a cast that's when I wrote my book. In 1967 that's when I started with the Amateur Athletic Union Boxing...refereeing. In AAU Joe Saunders was the head man for boxing and I did that boxing officiating all the way up to 1998 but they changed it to USA boxing.

(Q) Is there anything from the seventies to share about?
(Answer): That's when I was going all over the United States officiating all of the casino fighting. Oh I never

mentioned when the British came over here and fought the Sheriff's Department I was the Center Official. I had been to England three times and I mentioned that to Scotland Yards also and he officiated so much and I was the senior referee. There was a big boxing show in North Hollywood that I helped officiate. Arnold Swarzenegger was there and he even shook my hand.

The movie stars were there too the comedian, George Burns, Rochester he was with Jack Benny and we ate the same food everyday. I'll never forget they brought this little bowl of cherries or something or another and they said this was getting your mouth ready for the steak (chuckle). And they had all kinds of hors d'oeuvres and stuff out in the front and I couldn't see how people ate so much. They had oysters on the egg shells and shrimp and everything. And everything was so beautiful and they ate all of that and then could come and eat all that big meal, but we ate the same thing that they did ah ah when we were going to the job. But that was to bring it up to something that happened and she worked for Dr. Carson and we were waiting out there for our cars to come up. And while we were waiting this limousine pulled up and this white woman got off it and came around and bent down and pulled her dress up and mooned us. She was laughing (chuckle) and caring on and shaking her butt at us, and I said "I'll be darn." Laverne Peterson's car came first and she went on and off and mine came and I drove on up by her drinking and smoking cigars. They would auction off their cigars and all that kind of stuff. They treated us like real people.

Final memories and observations from D.L

As I sat down and broke bread with Soke I just listened to him talk. He shared with me how his being a leader and martial artist made a difference in the community he lived in. What he helped me to realize was that he was an influencer well before the term came to be known what it is today. Be it a family or community member that needed help it did not matter. Soke Peterson showed up, he was there for others.

While stationed in Bremerton, Washington Soke Peterson shared a story of a man that dated his sister and unfortunately domestic violence was involved. One evening while at his sister's home he advised the so-called boyfriend that his life expectancy would be short if he put his hands on his sister, Freida. Of course the fella denied doing so and asked who accused him of the abuse. Soke exercised self-control and discipline that is inherent in a disciplined martial artist. Soke returned to base and consulted with the base chaplain. Together they came up with a plan that involved law enforcement to help his sister. The abusive boyfriend was invited to a local hotel to meet Soke's sister. Shortly after entering the room true to form the so-called boyfriend attempted to assault his sister and was caught in the act. Law enforcement was waiting in the room. After he raised his voice and grabbed her the officers came sprung out of their location. They grabbed and arrested him without further incident. This was a testament to the patience and knowing when to respond a given situation.

Soke shared multiple stories of encounters with the Bloods and Crips gangs in Compton. The local gangs had multiple experiences where they came to realize that this man did not play. Soke did not fear them and they came to have a fearful respect of him. If Soke had to intervene and come to someone's rescue in the neighborhood they came to understand, do not mess with this man. When he told gang members to not cause trouble on his block and street overwhelmingly they complied.

Soke shared a story of how the veterans at the VFW Post in Compton extended a olive branch of sorts and made their facility available to the Bloods to use for one of their parties. The group was disrespectful and left a mess. They marked up walls and various surfaces in the club. The members of the post vowed to never make that mistake again. Sometime later at a dance held at the VFW Post for it's members some of the young gang members managed to intimidate the monitors at the door and got by them. However, when Soke was alerted of their presence and confronted them in the hallway, he gave them an option of the soft or the hard way. Soke made the first guy an offer he could not refuse. The gang member selected the path of least resistance...the soft way. They turned around promptly and walked out of the VFW club.

Soke told a story that one day after he picked up his laundry at a local dry cleaners, he headed toward his vehicle and saw a group of females. He got into his car and tried to back up but was surrounded by the group of female gang members. They blocked his way, taunted him and said, "You are that martial arts teacher and you think that you are bad." Soke had to get to work but they chose to instigate and prevent him from leaving. He said, "wait a moment," so he reached under his car seat and showed them the 38 caliber. Once he showed them what he was working with, they all backed up and he drove away. Today he will not allow a firearm anywhere near his vehicle or home.

Not only did Soke have encounters with notable figures in Compton but one small interaction also had an impact. His late wife, Clemencia (Esing), was a friend of O'shea Jackson's grandmother. The grandmother had an issue once when a man tried to perform a money shake down on her. Soke got word of her issue with the man. He walked down the street and had a conversation with the man. He convinced the man that he needed to disappear and the man chose to leave with haste. What Fred Peterson brought to his street and neighborhood was a caring and can-do attitude. Sometimes that is all it takes to be a difference maker in the community. Soke's memory of O'shea Jackson was that of a little boy smiling while he rode his tricycle down the sidewalk. That little boy would grow up to become one of the most impactful influencers in the world...Ice Cube...Straight out of Compton.

These are just a few examples of how a teacher of the martial arts can make a difference in the community should he/she choose to. Some amenities, benefits and burdens will at times accompany our walk in the martial arts. All in all, I would say that it is well worth the journey to be a leader wherever our training takes us. In life it sometimes becomes necessary to wear many hats in and out of the martial arts. Soke has many more stories like these we could have shared with you. In his own way, he has been a real life "Equalizer"of sorts.

Chapter Thirteen

Respect Earned and Given

Grandmaster Byron Mantack

As one of the pioneers of martial arts in the United States of America, Soke Frederick Peterson is a legend; a living legend, and I am honored to be able to call him a friend. He has taught me much about what it means to be a martial artist; however, to referring to him as one of my martial arts instructors, would be to dishonor him.

Soke, Great Grandmaster Frederick Peterson, is respected by many martial artists nationwide; and, particularly within the State of California, where he has officiated at many events sponsored and sanctioned by the Amateur Athletic Union (AAU).

Martial artists are respected by their peers, either for the rank they hold, the number of students they have, or for any number of other reasons; however, Soke Great Grandmaster Frederick Peterson has earned respect because of who he is. His straightforwardness, integrity, and overall personality are legendary; and, I must confess, he demands the respect of those around him, simply because he deserves it. Among the many awards and accolades that he has received over the years; was the presidential Champion Award, which I was honored to have presented to him, on behalf of the President's Council on Fitness, Health, and Nutrition.

--Grand Master Byron Mantack, The Martial Arts Academy

Peter Feeney

I owe a tremendous debt of gratitude to Soke Frederick Peterson for teaching me the martial art of Tai Chi Jitsu. It was such a great blessing to train under, and receive a black belt from, this supremely talented martial artist. Beyond that, I will always be deeply grateful for Soke Peterson's friendship and the friendship of my fellow Tai-Chi Jitsu black belts Thomas Hardie and (the late) Rickey Green. The years I spent training and studying with these men were among the best of my life. God bless.

Rev. DiAnn Johnson

I guess I was between 9 and 16 years-old and I would ride my bike over to his dojo in Compton. I would climb up on a lower level of the roof of the place that he had and I would watch him. To my knowledge I'm not sure that he knew that I was there or not but I would concentrate on the things that he was teaching. Then I would go home and I would practice. Later on in life when I met Chuck Norris, I guess I was about 19 or 20, I would work out in Chuck Norris's place at 6401 Wilshire Blvd. Now this was after being injured in the United States Post Office with a lower back injury. I would workout and I would remember the things that I saw as a kid at Master Peterson's place. Chuck Norris couldn't figure out what I was doing. He didn't know about it, he didn't know I was a strong competitor. I mixed what I learned at Chuck Norris's but kept the base of my fighting, my kata, weapons, everything from what I saw and learned at Peterson's.

Then later on when I started working with Master Jhoon Rhee and Master Joon Chung for Taekwondo I was doing the same thing. Combining all that I had learned but keeping what Master Peterson was teaching, that's my base. They never could figure out exactly what style I had because I had learned from the different ones and combined it. I was able to retire years and years later undefeated. I had never been defeated in kata, kumite or weapons. I even decided one time to go to a Kung Fu tournament and Kidd Jason was there and he watched me. I told him I was going to do a Taekwondo form and beat all of the kung fu katas and I did it. I say all of this to say I always kept the basis, my foundation was from Master Peterson. To this very day I am teaching and working with my 8 year-old great granddaughter and it is the same thing. I am teaching her his foundation. He touched my life from a kid all through my adulthood till I actually retired. You never know when you're doing something who's watching. I will be thankful to him forever.

Grandmaster Gustavo Martinez

When I was training in the eighties, Soke was the one who taught me the right way to do throws. He made a lot of difference in my life. He was very tough. He trained for real combat and street defense. Soke was the real McCoy. I couldn't believe his techniques were so simple but so effective. During those days in the early eighties I was driving from San Diego to Compton 2 to 3 times a week because I believed in what he was teaching. Even when I tried to make excuses about what I couldn't do he pushed me and encouraged me that there wasn't anything that I couldn't accomplish if I trained my body and my mind. I learned this from him very clearly.

He made a big impact on my life. He was definitely old school. I am a mechanic and sometimes I would pull a muscle in my back. I remember that he threw me around so much in judo that I feel like he fixed my back and put it back into place. He was a very tough person to train under. I also trained under GM Thomas Barro Mitose the son of GM James Mitose and he was not even half as hard as Soke was in training and practices. Soke was one of the greatest persons I ever met. Something very important I found out is that all of the techniques that Soke showed to me are very easy to meld with other systems. Soke showed me a lot of movements and a lot of techniques. I feel very fortunate to be taught by him.

Master Dunimus Nickelberry

I am eternally grateful for the discipline, the time in with Soke Frederick Peterson has imparted into my life, powerful tools have been developed though Tai-Chi Jitsu in which I have used to build a Martial Arts foundation. Dunimus, aka Willie Elam. 5th Dan

Grandmaster Steve Gallardo

As child growing up in the martial arts, I have met some very influential people and have trained under great ones well. During my days of competition, I met a very respected gentleman by the name of Grandmaster Frederick Peterson, it was during a tournament that he came up to me and advised me what I was doing wrong and what I could do next time to win. As I got older in my 20's I would meet him again while training with Robert Murphy and Compton Te Do Karate, that's when I was fortunate enough to study under both instructors. As years gone past, I would find that although I was becoming a great practitioner of the arts, I lacked true historic knowledge. Today I am still blessed to Say that I am still under his tutelage and reminded that there is still much I am learning about true martial arts and its origins. Soke Great Grandmaster Frederick Peterson is one of the most respected and influential men in the arts to this day, also a historian of the arts and who has served during World War II. I am proud to say I'm his student who's truly blessed to be under his wing.

Senior Master Tim Stewart

I have always thought of Soke Peterson as my grandfather in the martial arts, an example to emulate. As I grew and matured he became a friend whom I treasure, knowing him is one of the great honors in my life.

Grandmaster Kidd Jason

There was a tournament at Cal State Long Beach and Master Peterson had a physical confrontation with another martial artist outside by a catering truck. The site security came running up to assist and one of the security guys said that he was really fast like a cat and I said oh...Big Cat Peterson and the name just stuck. That name was put on him in person. Peterson was one of the first Black instructors that taught open martial arts. Everybody was doing the traditional arts like the Japanese. There wasn't that many Korean schools in the sixties and seventies but Peterson started teaching in the late sixties in Compton.

Peterson taught at a few locations in Compton. I remember Peterson rented a factory type of house near the corner of Alondra Blvd. and Atlantic Ave. near the 710 freeway. I taught weapons to his students there. One time I threw a tournament for him and we did a fish fry. It was a fish fry tournament, believe it or not. People who came out had free fried fish that he would barbecue. It was a Night Owl tournament, I was the one that kinda really got that out there, the Friday Night Owl tournaments. We did not want to mess with the Saturday tournaments but we were trying to get rated. A number of schools showed up, it was really good. We had a real good time. They tore the barbecue fish up. We wanted to do something different.

One time we through a tournament at the Compton Theater and quite a few schools showed up. Right after the grand championship match ended the cops came to raid the place. They thought it was some kind of militant thing. Peterson stood up to them and said I will take you to the superior court and I'll see you down to you drawls. Then Peterson and I told the cops to take a good look around and see how many black belts are in here. So they got real polite after we told them the tournament was nearly over. This was near the time around the riots and we de-escalated the situation. Peterson did not back down because he had been certified by the City of Compton to work with the youth. He held his ground and they eventually left. Peterson stayed active and he was even one of the top judges in the A.A.U.(Amateur Athletic Union) and much more. I honor him.

Grandmaster James Culpepper

I met Master Peterson in 1976 and who turned me on to him was my first instructor, Rev. DiAnn Johnson. I was with her and she promoted me to black belt so I came to him as a black belt and I trained with him at two locations including one on Alondra Blvd. When I first came there his main student was Big John Robertson. I came not long after him and I trained with Peterson a long time. Tai-Chi Jitsu is his own system and that's a name I was proud of.

Master Peterson had a lot to give especially for his wisdom, he comforted me and he took me on. I took grand champion at two of his tournaments. One was at Compton College and the other was at L.A. Trade Tech College and I won both times. I had to fight Big John at a tournament in Ventura, CA for the grand championship and he won but it was still a lesson to me. Mr Peterson told me one thing he said regardless of where you placed or how you placed always remember that you made an effort. He always told that to me, some effort was always better than nothing. I love him for that. I've made mistakes in my life but he coached me better right out of it.

When I had my last workout with him I told him that I found Steve Sanders and I want to go to BKF and he understood that. He said the more you have in your arsenal, your ability will grow. I will never ever forget that. He saved my life you know from DiAnn to Mr. Peterson to Steve Sanders those are the ones who made me what I am today. If it wasn't for Mr. Peterson I wouldn't even had thought about going for world champion, grand champion and all that. Those were just titles, I wanted to learn his art and Tai-Chi Jitsu is a unique art. It has judo, it has Jiu Jitsu, it has boxing and it's everything combined into one. So I created my system called All Options, Ken-Boc-Ryu. I took elements from DiAnn Johnson, Mr. Peterson and Steve Sanders/Muhammad, but I am so grateful that Mr. Peterson took time to share with me. I will always be a student of his. Mr. Peterson is a big part of the history in the making of me.

I got out of the Marine Corps in 1975 and those three instructors I mentioned are my impacts. My instructors are all Black. No Korean, no Japanese, no Hawaiian, or Filipino all my direct instructors were Black. DiAnn Johnson, Steve Sanders and Fred Peterson are all pioneers of martial arts and they are my background. If not for them I would not have learned the true value of the martial arts. From my understanding the martial arts originated in Africa. The kenpo is my base but Tai-Chi Jitsu was my ryu. I am honored to be a part of Fred Peterson.

Professor Frank DeGourville

During the eighties he used to teach out in his backyard. I used to teach in my backyard because I always had my dojo. Every three months or so he would always come through and demonstrate his Tai-Chi Jitsu. He was so dedicated, committed and so humble. Now that he has gotten older people don't give him the respect that he deserves as a Black man. Grandmaster Peterson is a historian, people need to know who he is. I travel a lot outside of the country and when I go places people know who I am and they respect me but I am nobody compared to Grandmaster Peterson.

Paul Pinckard

Soke "Big Cat" Frederick Peterson. He's a World War II Veteran and Great Grandmaster and Martial Artist who trained our soldiers in hand to hand combat in the Pacific. A great man.

Grandmaster Eric Lee

I met Grandmaster Peterson during the sixties. He judged me when I competed in the Golden Age of martial arts in this country during the sixties and seventies. I congratulate Soke Peterson for still going strong with his longevity in the arts. What I like about Peterson is that we appreciate history but understand what counts is what you do on the street. Do not be a slave to getting old. You can live a long productive life like him. I say life is always under construction and that is why Soke Peterson is still doing well at 96.

He was a really good judge when I competed. He was actually one of the pioneers. During those days when I first started competing mostly all of the competitors wore white gis. I was different when I came on the scene wearing a black gi but Soke did not have a problem with it. His judging, refereeing was all good during my competition days. I received a lot of positive energy from him.

Just by watching him I learned a lot and my life is richer. Many years ago I learned to always respect my elders in the martial arts and Soke I have a lot of respect for. He's been around a long time and he deserves respect. Soke still trains a little and I find that admirable at his age. His mind is strong. He keeps his self going because he has peace. Al Dacascos has a quote that I apply to Soke's life..."A turtle never goes anywhere unless he sticks his neck out." Soke is still doing it. He appreciates life and he has what he has because he worked for it. He is happy with his environment and he is at peace with his life. Soke has a lot of wisdom to pass on to the younger generations. He is a good guy. When I get to his age, I want to be as tough. Yes, I call him a friend too.

Lady-Lallaine Reed

The first time I met Soke GM "Big Cat" Peterson was in 2017 at the Shinjimasu Tournament in Banning. He was introduced to me as one of the oldest and greatest martial artists. I asked him what it takes to be a champion. He said, "Keep yourself in shape." Since then, I've been seeing him on martial arts events. I even took a couple of his Tai-Chi Jitsu Seminars. He invited me and my husband to come to Arizona and visit him. We went to his home in 2019. He welcomed us with great hospitality. He proudly showcased all his achievements and told us how his life was. Do you know that he was married to a Filipina? I guess I remind him so much of her. He is the most fit person I've met in his age of 95. He is mentally sharp and his eloquence is phenomenal. Some 50 year-old men would be such a bore next to him. As a martial artist, he is someone to definitely look up to.

Lori Hallmark

I love my Martial Arts Daddy! I need to go visit soon. If you want to learn some amazing history, just write to him and he will tell you so much. The man, the myth, the legend... Soke Grand Master Frederick Peterson.

I love you Frederick Peterson!

Grandmaster Albert Wilson

Master Peterson was one of my judo instructors at John Ogden's Judo School. I remember Peterson was hard on you. He didn't play around. He would constantly push you just like John Ogden did. He would constantly push, push you and would try to make you do better than what you were doing. He would always tell me when you get with those other belts you give them your best. You might not beat them but you give them your best. When you get back to the other ones your rank you can get them. I also noticed that he had a lot of respect for the dojo and he had a lot of respect especially for the mat. When you came inside the dojo it was strictly for the martial arts. He did not want you to disrespect the dojo or the mat. Soke wanted you to be focused when you were on that mat.

He and John were always trying to invoke you to do better than you were, to always do your best. I think he and John Ogden had the same motto in training. His motto was "A quitter is never a champion and a champion is never a quitter." He said I don't care if you lose just get up and do better next time. I had a lot of respect for him because he always pushed me. He was very serious about the martial arts. Peterson did not mind you learning karate along with the judo. He would encourage me to learn all I could learn. He did not put a lot of emphasis on trophies but he told me to just learn the martial arts and I told him I heard him and I respect him for that.

Rev. Orned "Chicken" Gabriel

I came to know Soke from the tournament circuit. He was always like an inspiration to me, always in my corner too at the competitions that I did. He was always there, he judged my forms, he always was fair and made sure that I did not get stabbed in the back. He was a fighter for Black folks and Black martial artists because we went through a time of prejudice and discrimination in the martial arts and we still are. He was a pillar in the Black martial arts community. I know he's a man of God, I know he's not into all of that false religion.

Always in the celebrations that we went to he was always outspoken, he was very courageous and confident. He did not take no stuff from nobody. Even at this late age last year we had a teacher's seminar. He came out and demonstrated at his age. He brought his wife with him and he showed some moves and stuff. I said look at this guy. He's got a lot of wisdom. You can't just find wisdom. You've got to get wisdom from God. It has got to be a gift. He has the gift of wisdom. He was on the battlefield and he's still on the battlefield.

Senior Master Emanuel Thomas, Esq.

I am excited that the World will get a glimpse at one of the greatest martial artist of our lifetime. Soke Fred Peterson has broken so many racial barriers and has been an inspiration to many martial artist such as myself. Congratulations Soke on your well Deserved biography.

Beyon Mahur Bey

The "Big Cat" "Great Grand Master" "Soke" "Judan" Frederick Peterson introduced me to my favorite form of "Montu Arts" (martial arts misnomer) called "Tae Chi Jitsu" in Compton Calif. around 1992. I received a 1st

Degree black under Him. He is still with us over 90 years young, still training, still instructing, the eldest Black Belt in the USA. Please Honor this Living Legend...Peace & Love.

Grandmaster Rey Leal

I got to know Soke Peterson during the days of my competitions on the tournament circuit. He was a very fair, competent and knowledgeable judge who was great to see in action. Much respect and honor Senior Great Grandmaster Frederick Peterson, Ooyahhhh!

Coach Apache Daklugie

Soke was a very good advisor to me. He took a liking to me right away. He didn't want to shake my hand. He said no handshaking for you, he wanted hugs because some people need that encouragement. I first met him at a gathering in 2011. He said a true martial artist has to do so with love. He said to me if you can't love them how can you teach? Soke Peterson encouraged me that people need hugs to make up for the love they had in the past. He would often welcome me to sit at his table. He and others looked forward to me playing the flute and sing some songs. He remembered when I was appreciated for my underground fighting and brutality and not for how I was supposed to be honored. Because of Soke and many other teachers like GM Mantack, they said I needed to get what I earned, my belts, plaques, recognition, fame and things like that. He really opened up some eyes toward me to being recognized and branded like others in the martial arts world. It touched my heart and he taught me that I could be more dedicated and that I could even conquer my enemies with love, that's what a true martial artist does. Soke told me that if I couldn't love my enemies then how could I love God. There was a time when I blessed Soke with some Shaolin prayer beads. He cherished the gift. He told me that I did not have to ask men for permission to do so he told me to go to God before man. He encouraged me in this way, he advised my mind and my heart. He knew that I needed that love to overcome that man of the past in order to become the man I am today.

Grandmaster Robert Temple

Over the years that I've known Mr. Peterson, he has always been encouraging to the Black Karate Federation. I've spoken to a couple of my BKF brothers and they shared the same experience. When the BKF attended his events he always acknowledged everyone and made sure you felt included and welcomed. In this Mr. Peterson has been consistent - my BKF brothers and myself count it a pleasure to have known and been encouraged by him.

Grandmaster Dennis Horton

A Few Words About Soke Grandmaster Peterson...
Soke Grandmaster Peterson is the standard that all masters of the martial arts should strive to achieve. He is an honorable man of God, a skilled and experienced martial artist, a family man, and he positively uplifts his community. During more than one of his lessons Soke Peterson reminds us, his students, that Jesus was a martial artist that trained his mind in preparation for the crucifixion and that praying the Rosary was not a Catholic practice, but a practice that should be used to unite humanity in a common belief of what is good and decent.

As a skilled martial artist, he served his country in World War II, the largest and most costly conflict this world has ever seen. Many debate the effectiveness of traditional martial arts in the contemporary world. To those that do I challenge them to survive what Soke has experienced using modern MMA ground fighting. Soke is a great grandfather that proudly brags about the brag worthy accomplishments of his family and you will rarely see him without his wife. He shows all of us masters that the best example of mastery does not begin in the dojo, but in the home.

Finally, Soke uplifts his community. He is an active instructor, a member of the local American Legion, a voice on the phone during the holidays, and a neighbor smiling and reminding you of the goodness in everyday of life. I still teach my students what Soke taught me is the most important lesson in all of martial arts, "courtesy and respect." It is this fundamental lesson that forms the foundation of all institutions. Soke means the father of all, or head of family. What better message could there be? Who else but a true Grandmaster could say it?

Grandmaster Deedra DeCoster

Soke Frederick (Big Cat) Peterson took the time to mentor me without me ever having asked him. He is an "Old School" Grandmaster with having the first dojo in the United States since the 1940's, whose wisdom and knowledge continues to be passed down in the traditional way of Tai-Chi Jitsu. One of the greatest moments in my Kenpo Karate and Traditional Martial Arts career, was about seven years ago, when he requested my presence to attend his testing in Lakewood, CA to introduce him personally and have me as a guest alongside his disciples and testing board.

What a great honor to continue to be available for the Tai-Chi Jitsu organization. With rich traditions, after introducing him to the masses, he approached the floor like a stealthy big cat as his presence filled the room. He took his time, then joined me on my right side, acknowledged his wife, and gently smiled. You could hear a pin drop as he recounted his journey from his military experience and his beginnings in Tai Chi Jitsu. His voice resonated with everyone. He timelines the lineage of Tai Chi Jitsu and introduced GM Athen Nelson Wha-Rung-Do Association, and my Sr. GM Clarence McGee (resting in power) of the Black Karate Federation. Soke also made the recommendation for me to hold a Seat on the Soke Council and, being welcomed by GM Bryon Mantack, I cherished his leadership. His entire leadership team is beyond reproach, and that speaks to true old school leadership. I am very grateful to have experienced it firsthand as it has aided me in shaping my role as a black female 10th-degree GrandMaster of the Black Karate Federation, Ken Wing Tai Ba/Kenpo Karate practitioner, and teacher. I will leave you with this original quote that I find this recount very befitting of GM/Soke Frederick (Big Cat) Peterson's commitment to his family, respect for his Sokeship and leadership standards, and his tireless commitment to Tai-Chi Jitsu and the Martial Arts throughout the years. "He is the wellspring from which American Martial Arts has flowed."

GrandMaster Deedra DeCoster

Dr. Jim Thomas

The one thing that really sticks in my mind is that there has always been in our country, even in the military and martial arts there's been and probably will always be racial divides for those that are ignorant. One thing that I remember as a kid and even through my journeys in Vietnam and the military there are still divides but oftentimes brothers became brothers regardless of who you were or where you came from, what color you were, what size shoe you were it didn't matter. One thing about the martial arts in his generation he had every right to be sour to what going in and what the White man and lot of other people had done to African Americans especially at that period of time in life. He overcame all of that it was never an issue. I was looked upon as a little boy and not as a little White boy. That kind of stuff is what triggered me in my memories.

There are a lot of things that we shared, a lot of stories and he could be talking to you one minute, be laughing and joking whatever. When he put that gi on and start teaching a class, you just don't get out of line. You don't talk out of place, it didn't matter who you are or what you do. He's just going to tell you just how it is. Not too many are like that left, that's awesome to me.

You know what was so funny to me and it almost brought tears to my eyes. This lady she was just full of smiles. You could tell that she was older and she was older than he was. We got our meals and she started salting her meal. She was salting the hell out of her meal. She just kept putting on salt and he ran over there and grabbed that salt shaker from her hand and was wiping off the salt because she didn't know any better. Nobody was really watching her. He caught on to that. He walked over there and he's brushing off that salt off of her food. Here the elderly taking care of the elderly, it almost brought tears to my eyes. To see the love and compassion in his eyes of him looking out for his big sister. And here he's something like 94.

Soke Professor Grandmaster Irving Soto

I came to meet Grandmaster Frederick Peterson in 1986 at a tournament in Escondido, CA. He came across as a graceful, respectful man like a gentle giant and he immediately became my friend. He still is my friend to this day. I conducted a hall of fame event in 1998 down in San

Diego, CA. I was having trouble getting some things done. I had to go through some channels. I received help from the mayor. I managed to get enough support to conduct the Golden Global International Martial Arts Hall of Fame for the very first time. Soke helped me to get through the channels. What I did for him was to get a charter, a Sokeship by writing to Japan so I could promote other masters but at the time he was the only one qualified for the honor on that occasion. He was the oldest and most qualified. The panel of grandmasters took a voted and all approved for Grandmaster Peterson to be promoted to Soke. He had a wealth of knowledge and it was determined that he was deserving of the honor. Not only did he learn traditional systems but he created his own methodology.

I have done a lot of work training police forces around the country , working with the military and work like that. Honestly a lot of people actually knew about him. One time I visited Jim Kelly a little before he died in or near Oceanside and even Jim Kelly said he knew of Soke and said he was a beautiful man though he had not met Peterson in person. That just shows you that other grandmasters know who he is. I went overseas one time and I was close to Istanbul and people knew who he was, Isn't that weird.

What makes him stand out to me, what makes this man unique is that he keeps it real. He never changes who he is. Many masters put a belt on and forget where they came from. This man keeps it like he was there yesterday. He's a great martial artist, he knows his technique. I have watched him when he does seminars. He knows his training. He knows his definitions, he knows his vocabulary. He knows what a teacher does on how to simplify. A grandmaster knows how to write, put a book together and talk about it.

Soke is like a celebrity. He illuminates the room when he walks in. There is no negotiation about what this man is and who he is. I am proud to know that I am his friend. I want to be like him when I grow up, even though I am no longer a kid. I want to be like him and live this long. We have to learn how to appreciate our elders, those masters who will not be here tomorrow and tomorrow will be leaving us. Then you forget where your lineage comes from because those are the guys that have history. The man has 8 decades of living and in my book he is a legend. In my book he will always be remembered as one of the tops in the world.

This is a man of knowledge and he's seen a lot. He has given me wisdom, enlightenment, respect, courage, love, integrity...he's a good man. Someone like Soke who is beautiful in heart, soul, spirit is who you want to take you kids to learn from. Any person could take their child to this guy and he could teach them. This man would teach them what is simplistic, knowledge, skill, love, respect for all the little things, this is what Soke Peterson is all about. I just want to say that I love him. He is an incredible man and he has got my support any place he goes. He defies the arts and he is there. The man served our country in war. He's like a hero that walks amongst the populations. There is no Superman. There is no Batman. There are no iconic Marvel magazine characters walking around the world. But there are people that walk around the world, maybe they don't have superhuman strength but they do have skill and he is one of those guys. You better believe it. He is a good man and that's why I love him, he is incredible.

Freddie Perry

Grandaddy was like a true Dad in many ways. He taught me that first it don't cost nothing to wave. And if you are going to be a ditch digger, be the best ditch digger you can be. I love you, you taught me how to tie a tie and how to be a man. I was in the best shape under your training. Granddaddy, Big Cat I'm named after you. I am proud to be just like you, my Dad and Grandfather...P.S....I am Little Cat.

Joe Scott

To the number one foundation in our family, we love you, very thankful for you, and all your soft gentle teachings. LOL. Love you, Granddad Soke Big Cat, Granddad Grandmaster, Grandmaster Granddad Frederick D. Peterson, Dr. Soke Peterson, aka the Granddad of Granddad's. I hope I didn't miss any of your titles or aliases. I didn't forget about the Jaguar. Love you.   Joe Joe--Joe Louis

William Perry

I am the eldest grandchild of Frederick D. Peterson. My siblings in order from oldest (after me) to youngest are: Frederick, Alphonso, Heather and Bobbie.

My grandfather goes by many names; Soke, Grandmaster, Sensei, Big Cat, Master, Coach, Ref, and Timekeeper, but to us, he is just granddaddy.

Of all my siblings only my brothers and I attended my grandfather's martial arts schools. Our training included weekend tournaments all over California. My grandfather would also use my brothers and me as assistants in his many exhibitions; throwing us across the mat, performing chokeholds and leg sweeps, all while whispering instructions on how best to land or perform the maneuver. His teachings continued at home. If my grandfather found my brothers and me doing something wrong he would either make us lie on our backs and look at our belts for minutes at a time (neck strengthening) or he would have us stand in a wide horse stance arms out in front of us and opening and closing our palms (try this one - your forearms will burn) while each of us counted to ten in Japanese over and over.

My first memory of my grandfather was when I was 5 or so. He drove from California to Sumpter South Carolina to pick up my dad (William Sr.), my mom (Cynthia), my younger brother (Frederick - named after my grandfather), and me. We all crowded into his car and he and my dad took turns driving to California.

My grandfather has been a strong influence in my life. As a young man, my grandfather was in the Navy and he rose to become a Chief Radioman. Once he retired from the Navy, he worked for the City of Los Angeles where he repaired and serviced police and firefighter radios. My grandfather would always work on electrical devices at home too. I would often find him using his trusty Simpson Multimeter. This tool always intrigued me and sparked my interest in technology.

Today, as the Chief Information Security Officer for the City of Hope Cancer Center, I often reflect on how watching my grandfather's tinkering on our home appliances led me to this 35-year career in technology.

My grandfather impacted the way that I dress. As many of you who know him know, my grandfather is a sharp dresser! He loves dressing for church and social events. One of his traits that I emulate today is wearing cufflinks with my dress shirts and striving to be half as sharp as he is. Granddaddy is our patriarch, our mentor, and our example! We love him!

Dr. Yolanda S. Brown, (D. Min.)

Tribute to Frederick Douglas Peterson from His Oldest Daddy has been a treasure in my heart as his first born. I have a picture of him in the U.S. Navy & a gift he gave me when I was installed at Blessed Sacrament Church in Hollywood with pastor responsibilities, have remained in my office to this day. Just as he describes his daughters as "priceless," Dad's invaluable contributions to my life have formed the "curae personalis" (whole person) that I continue to become as a child of God: Mind, body and soul. This Legacy of loving care and blessings have passed onto my wonderful marriage of 32 years with Leon, 7 adult children, 23 grandchildren and 11 great grand children. With an eternally grateful heart, Yolly.

Thomas Hardie

Soke Frederick D. Peterson has had an impact on many lives throughout his time on this earth. This was due in large part to the simple characteristic of respect. It is easy to receive but it works best when it is given. Soke had to earn respect against bullies on the streets of Milford, OH. He had to earn respect in the U.S. Navy even when all did not enter with an even playing field to speak of. When he sought work with the City of Los Angeles he had to earn respect as a minority in a not so diverse workforce. As a martial artist in and out of the ring, he had to earn respect of his peers and competitors and that he did. Because of the consistency of his character in instructing, mentoring, officiating, difference-making and more he earned the respect of many. The preceding comments are from individuals whose lives were touched by him in some way. A number of them are accomplished martial artists in their own right. The others are family members who know the intimate side of the man. What they all have in common is that they exemplify the respect held for Soke Frederick D. Peterson Jr.

We are grateful to all who have shared words of tribute and appreciation for how Frederick D. Peterson Jr. touched and impacted a few lives along his life's journey. This is indeed a benefit and by-product of giving, teaching and receiving respect. This much-needed quality and characteristic is in high demand. You can only imagine how close the nations of the world would be. How well all people could co-exist if we simply showed more love and respect for one another. Soke Frederick Peterson may not have done all in life that he wanted to but we say to him that we appreciate all he did give and how it benefits us still. From the sacrifices to the trailblazing and from the teaching to the role-modeling, we give him honor. He would encourage others to do the same. Do not wait till a loved one or friend is gone to sprinkle a little praise on them. If they are worthy tell them and allow them to enjoy it while they can see, hear and feel the joy that it brings.

A gospel song immortalized by the late, great Rev. James Cleveland sums up what this chapter is all about. Oftentimes opportunities are missed to tell someone how you feel about them when you can. One could leave suddenly and then your left thinking why didn't I speak up when I had the opportunity or express appreciation to the one sooner. This chapter was dedicated to letting Soke Frederick Peterson know that he can enjoy his flowers, his appreciation right now in the present. The following verses speak for me:

Give Me My Flowers

Give me my flowers while I yet live so that I
can see the beauty that they bring
Speak kind words to me while I can hear them so that I, I
can hear the comfort that they bring
Friends and loved ones may give me flowers when I'm sick?
Or on my deathbed, but I'd rather have just one tulip right
now, than a blanket full of roses when I'm dead
Give me my flowers while I yet live so that I
can see the beauty that they bring
Speak kind words to me while I can hear them so that I, I
can hear the comfort that they bring

A Journey Called Peterson

Soke was pronounced to the world in March 1925 he is
he is still found to be active over the age of 95;

No longer does he fly through the air or do high kicks
but that does not stop him from still teaching it.

He was a fan of baseball, played much back in the day
when he started in boxing it took him a another way.

He served in the Korean War and years before that
WWII

His service and that of others still benefits me and you.

Kempo through James Mitose via the 1st Marine
Raiders

Trained legit, was ready for foreign and domestic
invaders,

In 1947 on the boat, at the base and even in the city

He did not play but he taught others to be gritty.

He's seen much in his life, he says a lot hasn't changed
first look within the heart for priorities to rearrange.

Soke protected, provided and planted good seed, so
today his family is blessed with very little need.

With each day that he continues to live out his story,
encourages us to get along and give God the glory.

The bottom line is he has endured for many a season to
instill and teach us may very well be the reason.

In Soke's life he has not received all of his due. Yet he
endured as a shining example for me and you.

Your beginning does not determine your end
be the real deal, show respect and do not pretend.

Thanks for reminding and teaching us all for awhile
that honor and integrity will never go out of style.

--Thomas Hardie, February 2021

Chapter Fourteen

The Legacy Lives On

As of the Winter of 2021, Soke Peterson is still doing well. Yes he experiences pains here and there as you would expect for someone his age but he is still going strong. In fact if you ask him how he feels and he will likely say "I am feeling in top shape." His mind is phenomenally strong given his age of 96 years-young. His memory and recall of events many decades ago in his life is truly amazing. He remembers aspects of his life and this nation's history in intricate detail.

In 2020 Soke and I participated in a seminar together during the month of October in Fullerton, CA. We were even due to participate in another seminar at the U.S.A. Martial Arts Hall of Fame event in Atlanta GA. for Grandmaster Jim Thomas who conducts events all over the country. In fact, Soke Peterson had the pleasure of officiating Dr. Jim Thomas for the first time when he was a 6 year-old competitor at a tournament in New Jersey. In 2019 we both travelled to Akron, OH and La Mesa, CA. to participate in seminars. Not only was he acknowledged for being the most senior martial artist present but he was recognized as one of the oldest and active martial artists in the country.

I am quite confident that as long as God allows him to "Big Cat" will share his experience and his heart with anyone who will listen. Soke loves to give back in other ways by the reading of scriptures at St. Mary Magdalene Church, his place of worship in Gilbert, AZ. He enjoys faithful service at his church and is a consistent attendee and participant. In fact if you stay at his home on a Saturday or Sunday come prepared to go to church with him and Elida. Speaking of Elida, Frederick Peterson could not have a more loving, and supportive wife than he does in her. They understand one another and work well together as a couple. Although Elida Peterson is not martial arts-trained, Soke says she can take care of business because she is from Juarez, Mexico. The two of them have truly been blessed with one another.

Soke Peterson remains quite passionate to share and pass on knowledge and techniques to help the older and even the youngest generations of martial artists. This great man at his age even follows social media (Facebook). He is quick to acknowledge and point out correction if necessary on topics relating to the martial arts. After all, Soke Frederick Peterson is literally likened to a living, breathing, almanac on the martial arts in this country. He sees each day on earth as a gift from God and he is content to share and give back knowledge whenever he can. Giving back is a excellent formula for productive living.

Respect is still a big part of Soke Peterson's life. Do unto others as you would have them do unto you. This is a creed that he firmly believes in. Obviously there was time in his life when he could easily settle matters of disrespect with his hands, feet, elbows etc. During WWII he said the motto was "kill or be killed." You had to be ready to go extreme because our wartime enemies were not looking to make friends.

Even today despite his age Soke Peterson can still take care of business if he has to, I pray that he never has to. Soke will be the first to tell you that he cannot do a flying side thrust or a jumping crescent kick anymore. However he can teach you how to do them. As we know age is an opponent that has never been defeated. His specialty now is "Old Man Techniques" that are best suited for a martial artist of a well-seasoned age. There is no secret that martial arts are suited for the young when it comes to great feats of speed, agility and stamina. As Grandmaster Albert Wilson of San Do Kai Karate Do who trained in judo under Soke Peterson at John Ogden's School of Judo for a time shared with me "we cannot allow the things that we cannot do, prevent us from doing the things that we can do". Both Soke Peterson and GM Wilson are in definite agreement on this point in their lives.

From time to time Soke shares with me instances of disrespect that he experiences. Millions of people in this country today are the beneficiaries of those who sacrificed for this nation. His service and that of the men and women who proudly served and serve our nation deserve our respect. Martial Arts are known worldwide for self defense, personal development and respect but, it has to be taught as well as practiced. Appreciation and consideration for one another is easy to practice and not hard to teach. Our martial arts traditions should not ever lose the practice or principle of teaching respect.

We want to encourage all that no matter where you start your martial arts journey in life to not give up. For many of us it has become a life journey as it did for Soke Fred Peterson. Often times there is a rush to reach a certain plateau like that of obtaining one's black belt. As special of a accomplishment that is after reaching that level, one's deep knowledge and understanding is about to commence. Try not to be discouraged by challenges of life that can derail your course if you allow them to. A case in point, Fred Peterson as a 15 year-old earned $1.10/day during his tenure at the Belvedere Hotel in Cincinnati, OH. No longer does he have to work for pennies on the dollar. Today he is retired after 42 years of combined public and military service to various cities, states and the nation. No matter how long it takes, train and enjoy your personal journey in the arts or whatever discipline brings you joy in life because you will reap if you sow.

Soke Fred Peterson did not allow disadvantages and racial inequalities in life to keep him from enlisting and serving with distinction in the U.S. Navy. This man also did not even allow being denied certain opportunities in and out of the martial arts to deter him from great accomplishments. He certainly did not allow being raised as an orphan to determine what his future would hold. Soke Peterson went for it and subsequently has had an eventful and amazing life up to this point. All will not agree with everything he says or does but this man will speak his mind and you will actually learn from him if you take time to listen.

It was mentioned early on in this biographical study that each time you sit and have a conversation with him it is likely you will get a different nugget and learn something new. For this is the reason that you are reading this book right now. If I had not cut it off when I did, no telling when this story would have been completed. He continues to recall story after story. Soke Peterson has an amazing and detailed plethora of stories to share and hopefully there will be other opportunities to do so while he remains as one of our living national treasures. Today when one goes to sleep there is no telling what you will wake up to. Our world can go from peaceful to volatile in a heartbeat. It is amazing to see and utilize all of the technological advancements that have been made over Frederick Peterson's lifetime.

Unparalleled successes that many could not have even imagined have occurred. Yet heretofore despite all of the great and phenomenal accomplishments that have been made, we collectively as a nation remain socially and spiritually-malnourished as we relate to one another. Though progress has been made we have much more work to do as a nation to become the best version of who and what we can be. If we would just embody a mutual reciprocity our potential outcomes would be immeasurable. Even though these are challenging and sometimes disturbing times in our nation right now those who stay ready, do not have to get ready. This is part of what Soke Peterson's life has been about staying ready during the time of war and relative peace.

Soke Fred Peterson is a survivor who can teach self-defense through the martial arts as well as self-preservation by way of the life principle of love. He strongly believes in the golden rule, a scripture in the bible found in Matthew (7:12) NIV states "So in everything, do to others what you would have them do unto you." Love and respect will go a long way to fix many of the ills in this world if all are taught and committed to its practice. Our nation is truly in need of more respect given and received at this juncture in our history. When he is introduced and recognized at events in which he attends, Soke expresses his love for all people.

Undoubtedly, Soke is especially fond of martial artists and always stays ready to lend encouragement to them. If you combine his boxing background with his martial arts training and teaching, Soke Peterson has over 80 YEARS of martial arts EXPERIENCE to date. He is thankful to be alive and remains eager to share the wealth of his life experience to help others. Not long ago Soke Peterson shared with me that he has been through a lot. Some of the things he saw and some of the things he did would have taken most people out of here. He acknowledged that he is only still here by the grace of God. We certainly hope that his story has informed, inspired and motivated you to stay ready in life. His journey from the orphan to the Soke has been long and painful at times, but overall it has been a genuinely-rewarding and eventful one.

It truly has been a honor and a privilege to have worked on this project. I personally learned a lot about the process of chronicling the life of an individual with such a rich background and history. Patience, discipline, perseverance and respect are necessary intangibles for this type of effort. These are also the characteristics of Frederick Douglas Peterson Jr., born in the town of Talbotton, GA whom many people have come to love and respect worldwide. Much thanks to all who took time to share history, stories and words of encouragement to the Soke.

On behalf of Dr. Danny Layne and myself Thomas Hardie, we give much thanks and love to all who contributed by being a part of Frederick "Big Cat" Peterson Jr.'s life journey and story in some way. As much as we have spent time studying his life adventures and history it could not have been without the countless individuals that influenced him or were influenced by Frederick Douglas Peterson Jr. Whether you acknowledged him as Steward, Seaman, Radioman, Petty Officer, Chief Petty Officer, Sifu, Sensei, Master, Big Cat, Grandmaster, Great Grandmaster, Soke, Doctor, Professor, Sir, Friend, Cousin, Uncle, Great-Great Grand, Great Grand, Granddaddy, Daddy or Fred, we take time to say *Thank You*.

The Genealogy

1. Born March 3, 1925--Frederick Douglas Peterson   Jr.
DNA: 35% Great Britain which includes Scotch-Irish (Grandfather on mother's side was Scotch Irish (Albert Gibson) Talbotton, GA

> Percentages of multiple ethnicities:
> a. 50% Congolese
> b. 19% Ivory Coast-flash-Ghana
> c. 14% Nigeria
> d. 9% Cameroon/Congo

Trace amounts
> a. 8% other African and other European

2. Parents
> a. Mother-Fannie Mae Gibson-Peterson
> b.Father-Frederick (Fred) Douglas Peterson   WWI Veteran

3. Great Grandparents and Grandparents
> a. Great(x3)Grandfather-(Mother's side) President Thomas Jefferson via oral story-telling
> b. Great Grandfather-Robert Alexander Ware
> c. Great Grandmother-Mary Francis Blanton
> d. Grandfather-Albert Lamar Gibson
> e. Grandmother-Anne Peterson
> e. Mother-Fannie Mae Gibson
> f. Father-Frederick (Fred) Douglas Peterson Sr.
> Grandfather on Father's side - Robert Jerome Peterson

4. Siblings
> a. Sister-Frieda Mae Peterson-Walker

b. Brother Robert Jerome Peterson

5. Known Relatives

Gibson Family (Tallbotton, GA)

Holt Family (Both White and Black) Talbotton and Junction City, GA.(owner of Railroad-Coffin Makers-liquor and many homes in Box Spring, GA)

Seth Thomas (uncle) Maker of Clocks all over the world.

Jones Family-Ben and Sara (Father and Mother) and Mitchell (children) Ruth Jones-Grant Nantucket, MA. Tabita Jones-Cincinnati, OH

Elaine Phillips, Butler, GA. Lyester Jones-Mitchell-Junction City, GA Biece (Sister) Nobel Mitchell(husband) Dorothy Jones-Georgia Elaine is mother of cousins Frederick, Frederick Mitchell-cousin Michael and Lisa, Michael-Warner-Robins, Georgia, Lisa

Relatives

Freida Mae Walker (sister) Seattle, WA. (Children) Leathia, Onedia, Carmen (deceased)

Theresa, James Jr. Cecilia

Clemencia Codia-Peterson (wife) 54 yrs.

Tacloban Leyte, PI. Born in Borongan Samar, PI

Mother-(nana and tata) Coridad and Eugoro Codia

Sister: Deding or Matilde

Parents and sister spoke only BA Sayan (PI language)

Uncle: John Codia

A number of their nephews and nieces are from in Borongan, Samar.

6. Children

a. Yolanda Brown-born in Tacloban Leyte May 10, 1946

b. Cynthia Jackson-born in Tabon, Kavite, April 14, 1948.

c. Rose-Mary Buckner-born in Portsmouth, VA, Naval Hospital May 10, 1950.

7. Grandchildren (15) of: Yolanda Brown, Cynthia Jackson and Rosemary Buckner: Yolanda Madden, Charles Madden

Joann Scott, Jo Jo Scott. The Brown boys

Cynthia Jackson: William, Frederick, Heather Perry

Alfonso Perry,

Cynthia Jackson's children

Bobbie Jewel Jackson and Andre

Around three or four Brown children, Leon Brown (retired) Los Angeles Sheriff.

Approximately forty or more Great Grandchildren by the above and children of Rosemary Buckner.

Namely Robin and Maigon (Robin is a doctor of Theology and Maigon is a English Teacher at Da Vinci Communications, LA, CA.

Approximately, eight Great, Great Grandchildren. All names I do not know. My wife Clemencia (Esing) passed away after 54 years in September 1999, in Compton, CA at 1320 S. Poinsettia Ave, Compton, CA after which I moved to Big Bear, CA for approx. 3 years. And then to Victorville, CA for approximately two years, Cherry Valley, CA until moving to present home at 4296 E. Spawn Lane, Gilbert AZ.

As of this writing, Frederick D. Peterson Jr. is the proud patriarch of his family with 3 daughters, 15 grandchildren, 42 great grandchildren and 8 great-great grandchildren in his bloodline.

172

Photo Gallery

From the navy uniform to the karate gi, Chief Petty Officer and Soke Fred Peterson is still looking sharp after 77 years of combined public service and teaching taken recently during time in Arizona.

Chief Petty Officer Frederick Peterson and his lovely wife
Elida Peterson pose with Ms. Arizona at the Mesa Veterans
Day Parade 2019. Chief Peterson served as a honorary parade
marshal on a beautiful November day in Mesa, AZ.

Soke Fred Peterson was honored as a Supreme Great Grandmaster at the Gedatsukai Master's Belt and Awards Ceremony with Thomas Hardie and other masters from the Eastern United Sates in May 2019 in Akron, OH..

This picture features the beloved Eleanor Roosevelt, her husband, the United States only four-term elected, President Franklin D. Roosevelt and Dr. Mary McLeod-Bethune. She was an advisor to Pres. Roosevelt on Negro Affairs. She was a close friend of Mrs. Roosevelt and Fred Peterson's foster mother.

Teenage Frederick Peterson who was an undefeated boxing champion in his weight class in the South Pacific during the early to mid 1940's. He competed in a number of unsanctioned boxing matches called "Smokers."

This is a picture of two mules, Maud and Doc. One mule is partially obscured by the other. Standing alongside is Frederick's foster uncle. One of the two mules was sent to meet young Frederick when it was time for him to walk home after grade school in Milford, OH. As referenced earlier in this biography the horse knew exactly where to go and wait to accompany the young Peterson home.

Frederick and Clemencia Peterson as a young
newlywed couple during the 1940's. She did not like
the physicality of boxing and was concerned about his
safety. She gave him an ultimatum to choose her or
boxing and he chose her.

Fred Peterson's daughters (L to R)....Rosemary, Yolanda and Cynthia with his late wife, Clemencia who he shared over 50 years of marriage.

Chief Petty Officer Fred Peterson (left-center standing) with some of his friends and the surviving ship stewards he served with during their 50 year reunion during the 1990's in Norfolk, VA.

Fred Peterson taking a break from one of the many boxing and mixed martial arts events he worked for the state of California. His referee and timekeeper career spanned 42 years.

Fred Peterson as an instructor for the U.S. Navy
Class A Radioman School in San Diego, CA 1963

Former world boxing champ Sugar Ray
Robinson was a friend of Fred Peterson. Both
taught boxing to youth in the City of Los
Angeles.

Laila Ali, the five-time, undefeated title holder and the daughter of Muhammad Ali was one of many Southern California boxing champions that Fred Peterson helped train when he lived in high altitude city of Big Bear, CA.

TIMOTHY "DESERT STORM" BRADLEY
UNDEFEATED WBC JR. WELTERWEIGHT CHAMPION OF THE WORLD

Former World Welterweight Boxing Champ, Timothy Bradley was a student of Fred Peterson. Bradley gave up training in Tai-Chi Jitsu to pursue boxing and reportedly said to Soke, "What do you think of me now?" at a boxing match that they both attended. Soke Peterson responded, "I can still teach you more self-defense!"

Photo on Soke's wall of "The Greatest" Muhammad Ali, the former three time Heavyweight Champion of the World. While on a parade float in the City of Compton, while Soke and students of Tai-Chi Jitsu demonstrated for the crowd, Ali signed this photo.

Soke Fred Peterson and other old school martial artists with Grandmaster Kidd Jason, Grandmaster Eugene Sedeno and the "Fighting Grandpa" who Soke Peterson competed against multiple times at tournaments in Las Vegas, NV. back in the 1970's.

Photo taken at the President's Champion Awards hosted by Grandmaster Byron Mantack (right center) featured Soke Fred Peterson (left center), Cynthia Rothrock, Donnie Williams, Dr. Jim Thomas, Larry Spears and other accomplished masters of the martial arts during the Summer of 2018 in Chula Vista, CA.

Soke Fred Peterson and one of his black belts, Sensei Sankara Frazier in the Compton Blvd. dojo back in the 90's. Soke assumes the position of the fighting cat stance of Tai-Chi Jitsu.

This picture of Fred Peterson in the U.S. Navy & a gift he gave his eldest daughter Yolanda Brown after she was installed at Blessed Sacrament Church in Hollywood with pastor responsibilities. It remains in her office to this day.

At a Black Belt Hall of Fame Awards Banquet in 2019, Soke Fred Peterson (center) and Gordon Richiusa (right) made the event even more memorable for Jeff Rombout (left) the first Heroes' Hearts Inc's first Heroes' Helping Heroes scholarship award winner. "It was on this night that I met Soke Peterson. It was also the night, I believe, I met the man who taught my Pearl Harbor survivor Marine father martial arts, on board a ship off the coast of Okinawa," said Gordon Richiusa, Director of Heroes' Hearts Inc.

Soke Fred Peterson and Grandmaster Steve Gallardo in their fighting stances from Tai-Chi Jitsu and the Kenpo Karate Connection respectively. The two were award recipients at the October 2020 U.S.A. Hall of Fame Ceremony in Fullerton, CA.

Teacher Fred Peterson and disciple Thomas Hardie perform the basic Tai-Chi Jitsu bow as Grandmaster Steve Gallardo and Soke Grandmaster Robert Murphy look on during visit to Gilbert AZ.

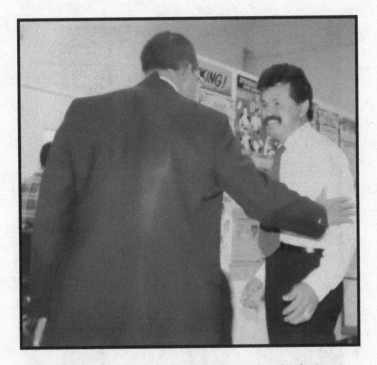

Soke Fred Peterson and Grandmaster Danny Rodarte welcome each other at an event in Whittier CA.. The two men started the Stars Full Contact Fighting Circuit in the United States in the 1980s. This circuit featured such renown competitors as Alvin Prouder and Benny "The Jet" Urquidez.

Soke Frederick Peterson is with his friend Dr. Jim Thomas who Frederick Peterson actually officiated as a young boy in a tournament many years ago. Dr. Thomas hosts the U.S.A. Hall of Fame events in various states throughout the country. The two are together here at an awards banquet during the Summer of 2018 in Chula Vista, CA.

Australian-born actor and martial artist, Richard Norton is flanked in this photo by Soke Frederick Peterson (L) and Dr. Danny Layne (R) at a Hall Of Fame banquet in Southern California. Mr. Norton appeared in several films and television shows and was in and out of the martial arts.

Gold Sash High Honors Council awards presentation conducted in the Chinatown District of Los Angeles, circa 2015. Seated from Left to Right: Grandmaster Albert Wilson, Soke Fred Peterson, (late) Professor Hugh McDonald, and (late) Grandmaster Ted Tabura. Center with red sash, standing in back row is Soke Robert Murphy along with other grandmasters from Southern California area.

The Peterson Family striking a pose together during the 1950's in Portsmouth, Virginia. Fred Peterson is with his lovely wife Clemencia and their three beautiful daughters L to R, Yolanda, Cynthia and Rosemary.

The Peterson Family photo featuring four generations that has since expanded to five generations strong. From Fred and Clemencia along with their three daughters, the family has grown to at least fifteen grandchildren, forty-two great grandchildren and eight great-great grandchildren.

A meeting of grandmasters, all friends, at the Champions Award ceremony and banquet in 2018 include (left to right) Orned "Chicken" Gabriel, Irving Soto, Frederick Peterson, Eugene Sedeno, and Gus Martinez. The event was hosted by another grandmaster friend (not pictured) Byron Mantack in Chula Vista, CA.

Fred Peterson as a Communications electrician for the City of Los Angeles. He serviced equipment from San Pedro to the Valley for the city, one of only two Blacks able to work in the department.

Frederick Douglas Peterson Jr.,..One of our greatest living legends today...Thank you for not only living and contributing to Black history, martial arts, and Naval history, but to U.S. and World history as well.

CPSIA information can be obtained
at www.ICGtesting.com
Printed in the USA
LVHW042322190421
684947LV00002B/17